The Franco-Spanish War:

the Sieges of Lleida

from 1644 to 1647

The Franco-Spanish War:

the Sieges of Lleida

from 1644 to 1647

Pierre A. Picouet

The Pike and Shot Society

The Pike and Shot Society
16 Cobbetts Way
Farnham
Surrey
GU9 8TL

Website: www.pikeandshotsociety.org

First edition, published 2014
Copyright © Pierre A. Picouet

Printed by Joshua Horgan, 246 Marston Road, Oxford, OX3 0EL

ISBN 978-1-902768-51-9

Front Cover: Detail from *Lerida en Catalogne*. (© Fons Sol- Torres / Universitat de Lleida)

Rear Cover: Detail from *Plan of the 1645 Siege of Balaguer* by the sieur de Beaulieu (1695) Institut Cartogràfic de Catalunya).

It is well that war is so terrible,
otherwise we should grow too fond of it.

R.E. Lee, 1862

Acknowledgements

The author wishes to express his thanks to Susana Pombo and Pavel Hrnčiřík for their encouragement, help and useful comments.

Contents

List of Illustrations and Maps

Figure 1: The relief of the fortress of Lleida by Peeter Snayers (1592-1667) (© Prado Museum)

Figure 2: The city of Lleida by the sieur de Beaulieu (1668) (© Fons Sol- Torres / Universitat de Lleida)

Figure 3: Undated engraving of Lleida showing the old bridge over the Segre river

(© Fons Sol- Torres / Universitat de Lleida)

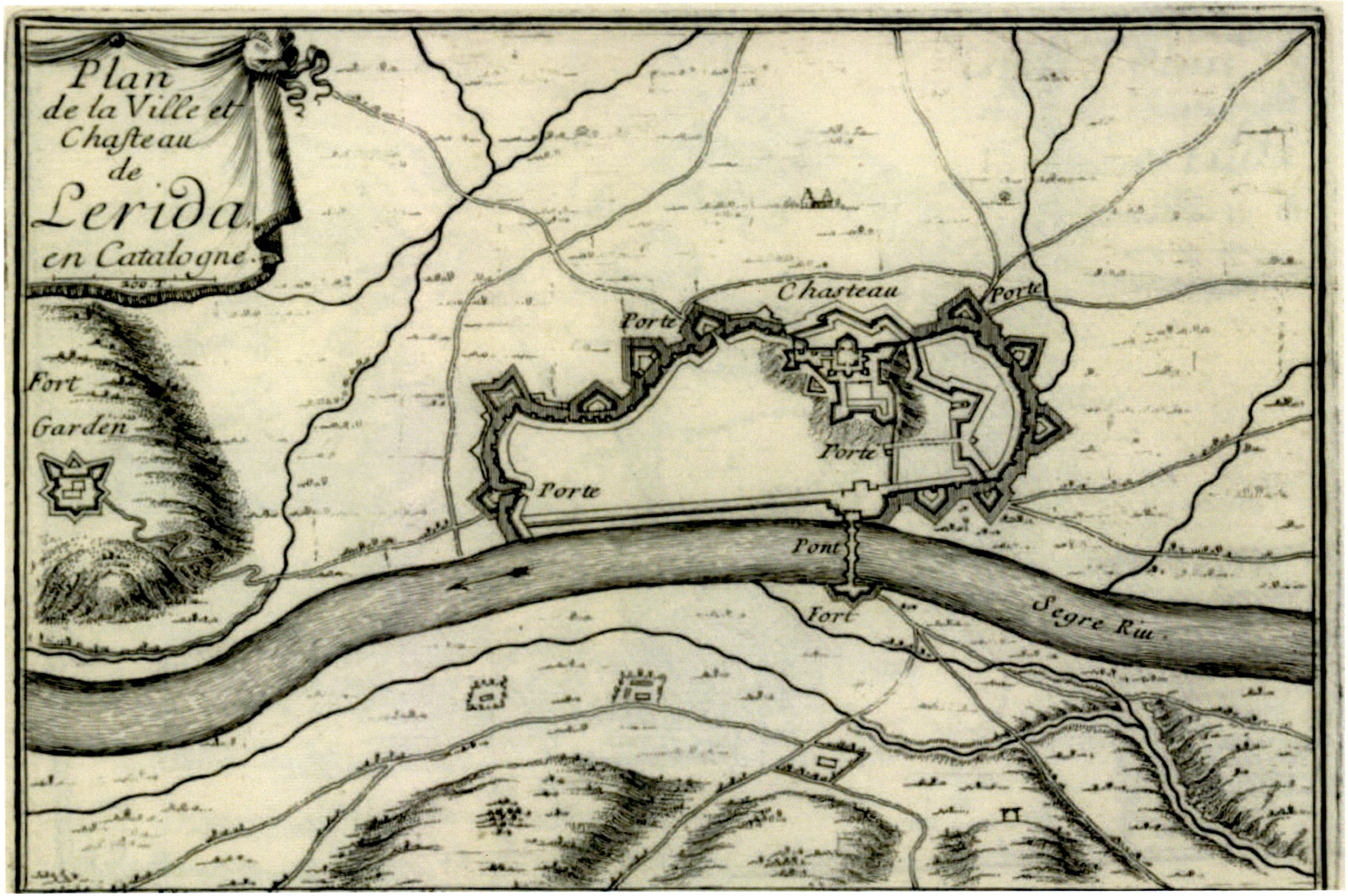
Plan
de la Ville et
Chasteau
de
Lerida
en Catalogne
Chasteau
Porte
Porte
Porte
Porte
Fort
Garden
Pont
Fort
Segre Riu

Figure 4: Plan of the town and fortress of Lleida by the sieur de Beaulieu (1668) (© Institut Cartogràfic de Catalunya)

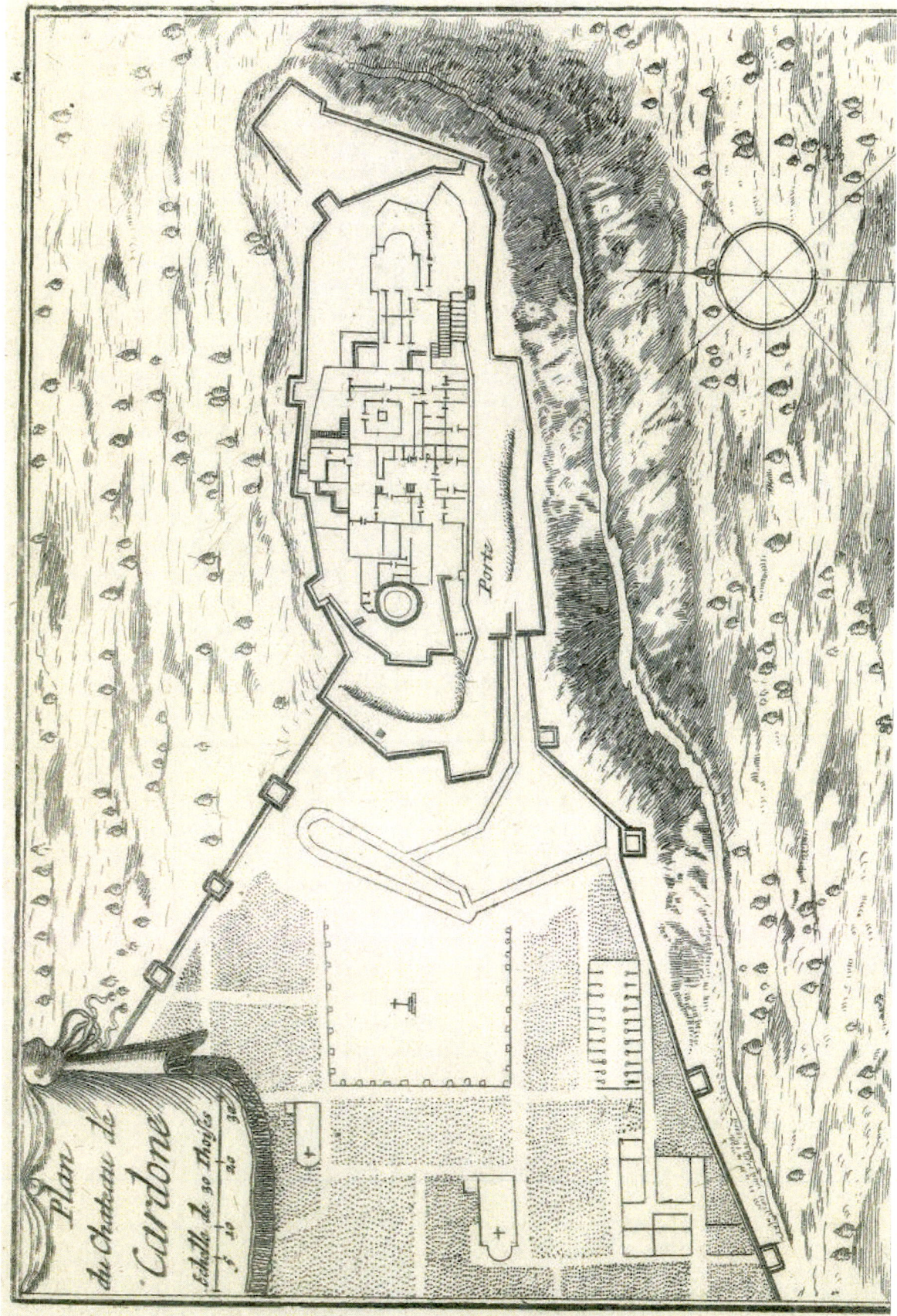

Figure 5: Plan of the fortress of Cardona by by the sieur de Beaulieu (1771) (© Institut Cartogràfic de Catalunya)

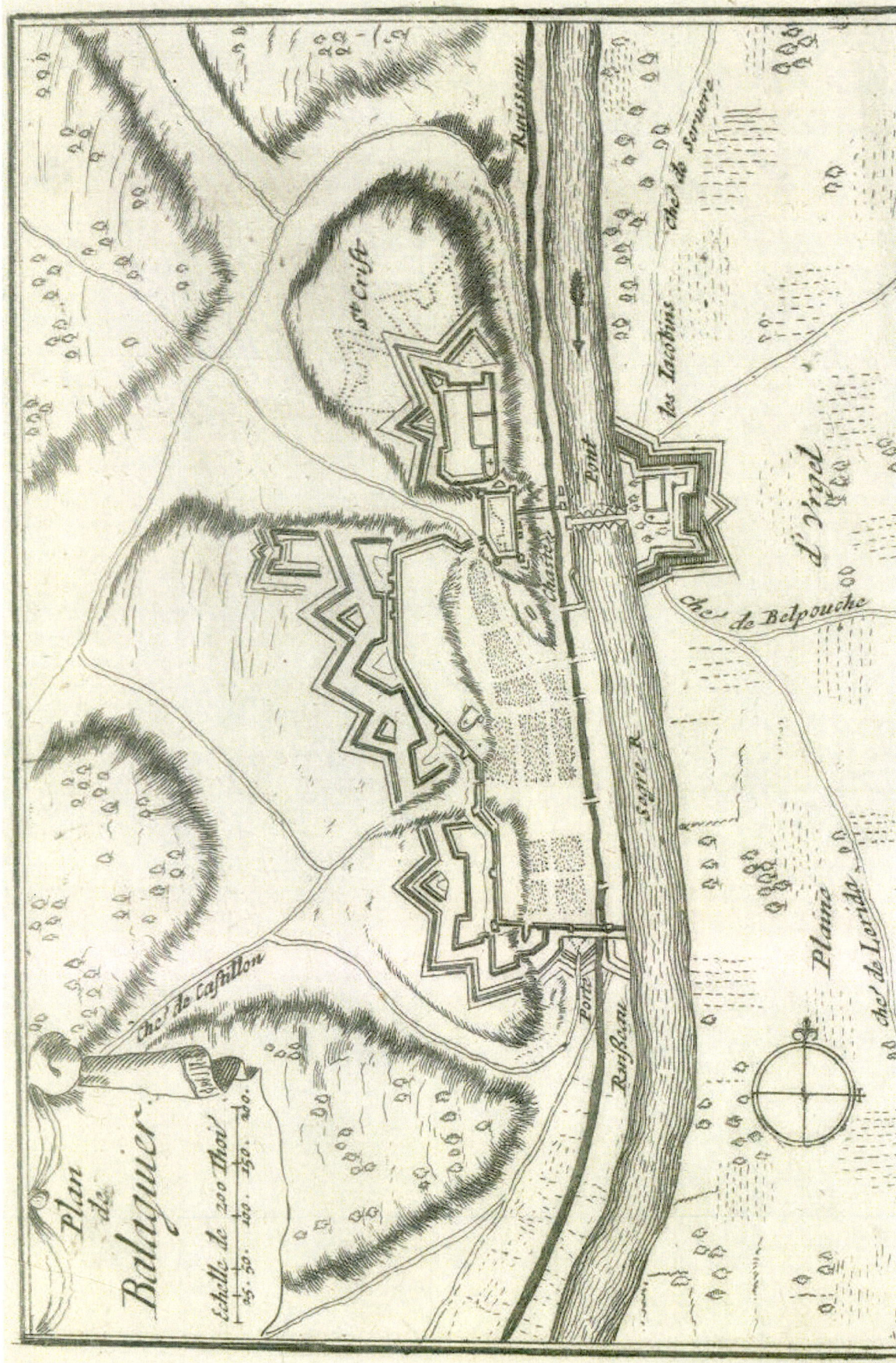

Figure 6: Plan of the town and fortress of Balaguer by by the sieur de Beaulieu (1771) (© Institut Cartogràfic de Catalunya)

Figure 7: Plan of the town and fortress of Cervera by by the sieur de Beaulieu (1771) (© Institut Cartogràfic de Catalunya)

Figure 8: Plan of the town and fortress of Ager by by the sieur de Beaulieu (1771) (© Institut Cartogràfic de Catalunya)

Figure 9: Plan of the 1645 siege of Balaguer by the sieur de Beaulieu (1695)

(© Institut Cartogràfic de Catalunya)

Figure 10: The battle of Sant Llorenç by the sieur de Beaulieu (1694)

(© Institut Cartogràfic de Catalunya)

Figure 11: *Lerida en Catalogne*, an undated contemporary print of the 1647 siege of Leida (© Fons Sol- Torres / Universitat de Lleida)

A. Caualier, et baterie.

B. La Magdelaine paroiße.

C. Porte de la Magdelaine

D. L'euesché.

E. l'Eglise Epiſcopalle.

F. Caualier, baterie.

Figure 11a: *Lerida en Catalogne,* detail (© Fons Sol- Torres / Universitat de Lleida)

G . la grande Tour .   K . Magazin de guerre .
H . Gallerie du Donion .   L . Fauße porte du Donjon .
I . la Cuisine d'Aragon .   M . la Ville haute .

Figure 11b: *Lerida en Catalogne,* detail (© Fons Sol- Torres / Universitat de Lleida)

Figure 11c: *Lerida en Catalogne,* detail (© Fons Sol- Torres / Universitat de Lleida)

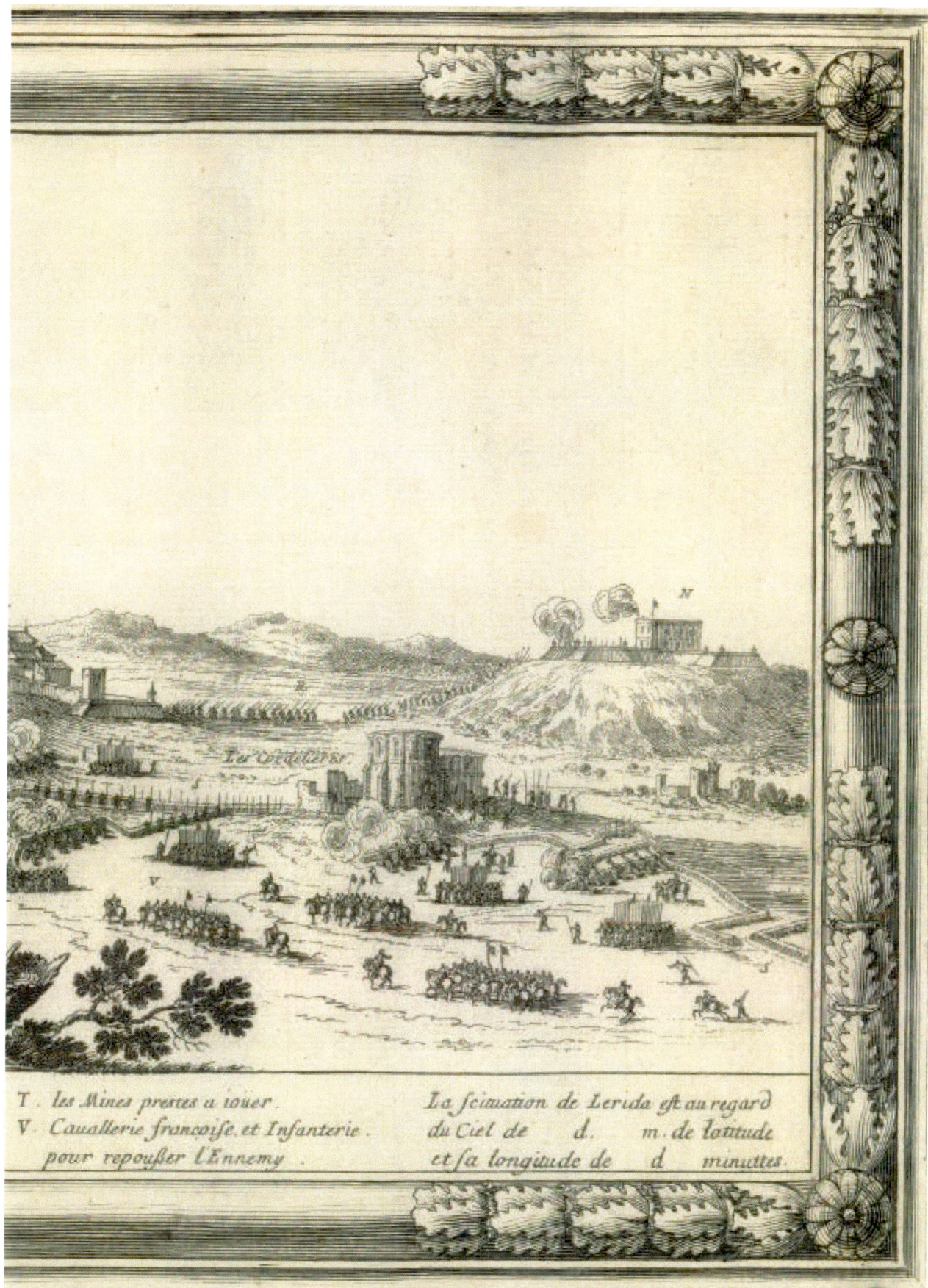

Figure 11d: *Lerida en Catalogne,* detail (© Fons Sol- Torres / Universitat de Lleida)

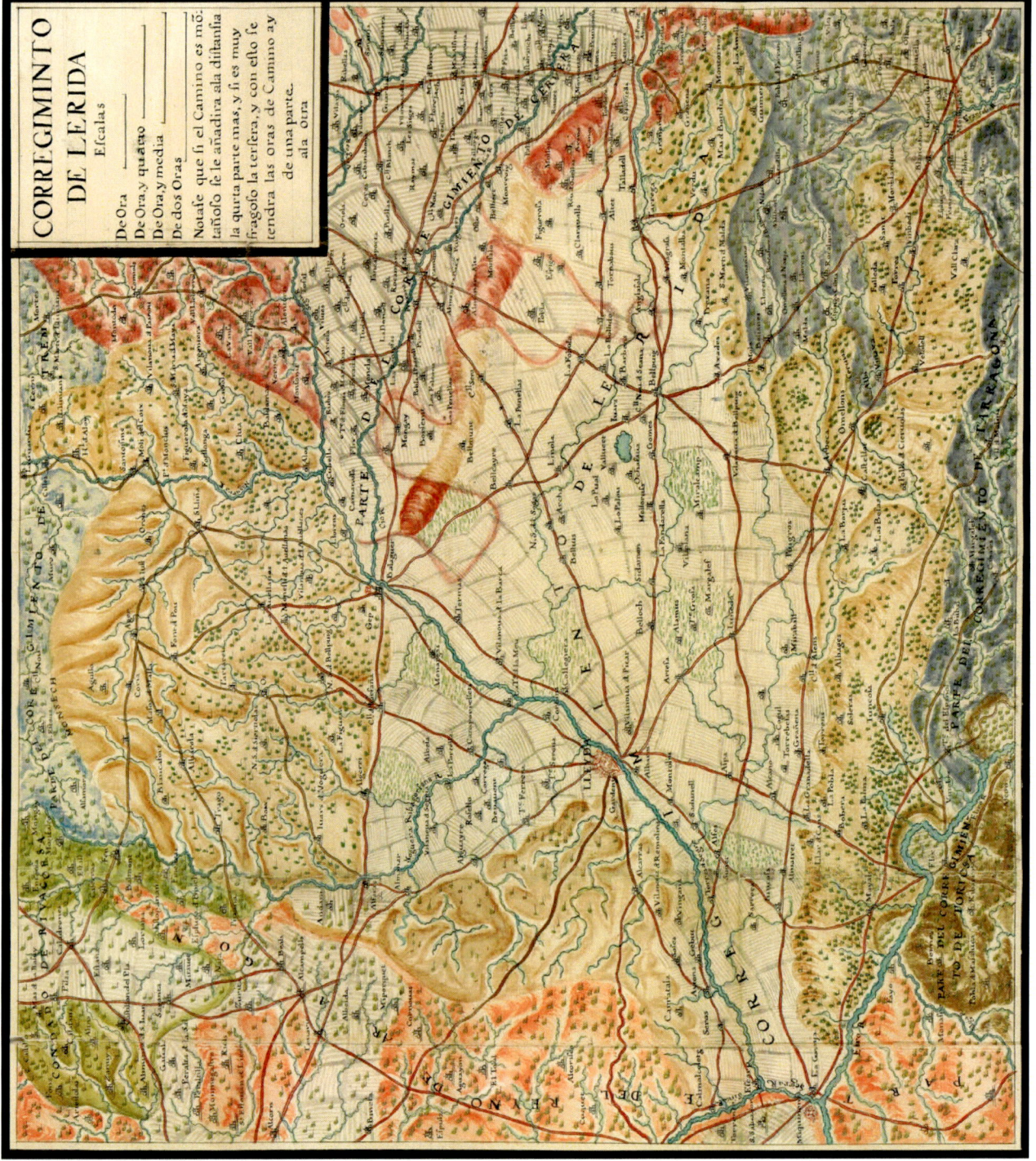

Figure 12: The region of Lleida from *Corregimiento de Lerida* (1716) by the comte de Darnius

© Institut Cartogràfic de Catalunya

Map 1: Map of Catalonia and the County of Roussillon at the end of the 17th century, showing the main cities. Cities in red were mostly in Spanish hands and cities in green in French or Catalan hands.

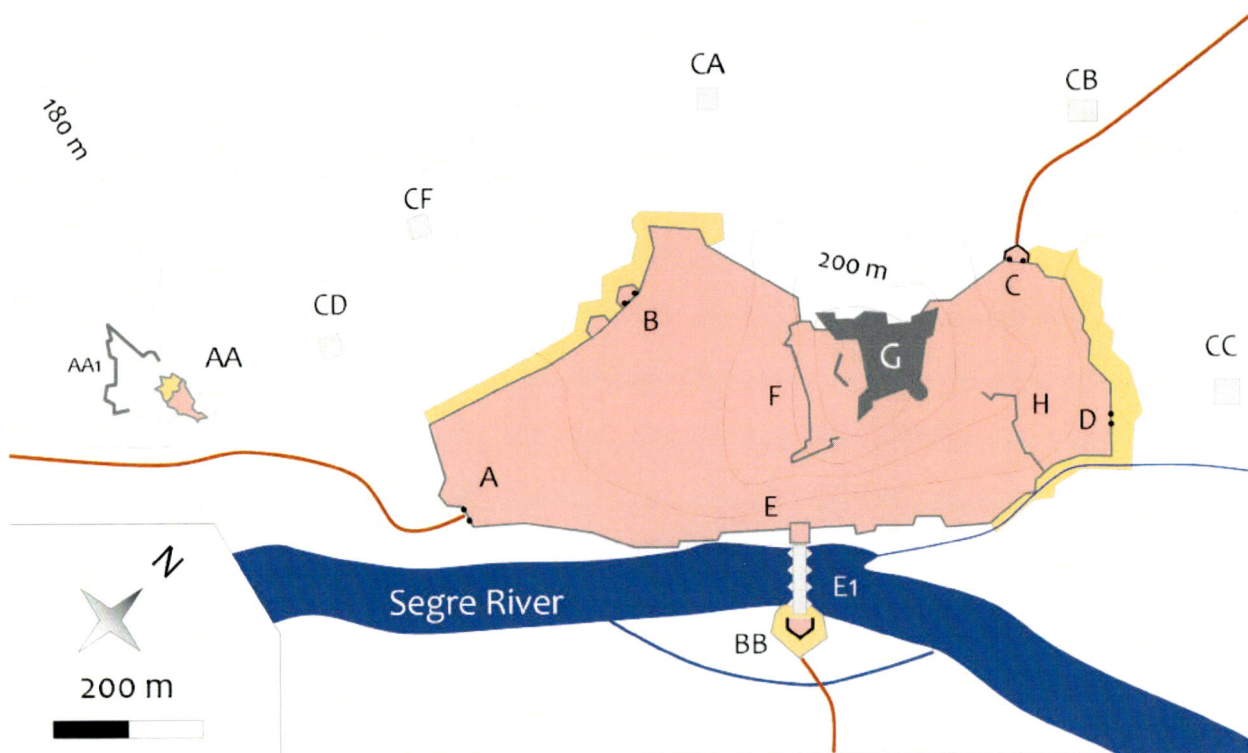

Map 2.1: Details of the city of Lleida, 1643–1648

A: Gate of San Antonio
B: Gate *de los Boteros*, covered by a bastion
C: Gate of the Infantes, covered by a bastion
D: Gate of San Espiritò, probably covered
E: Tower/door of the bridge. The bridge is made of stone (E$_1$)
F: Old medieval wall reinforced by Brito
G: New fortress of Lleida
H: New bastion of the Magdalena made by Brito

AA: Castle of Cardeny. New horn work (AA$_1$)
BB: Half-moon of the Cappont
CA: Convent of San Juan
CB: Convent of San Francisco
CC: Convent of Santo Domingo
CD: Convent of the Capucines
CF: Windmill

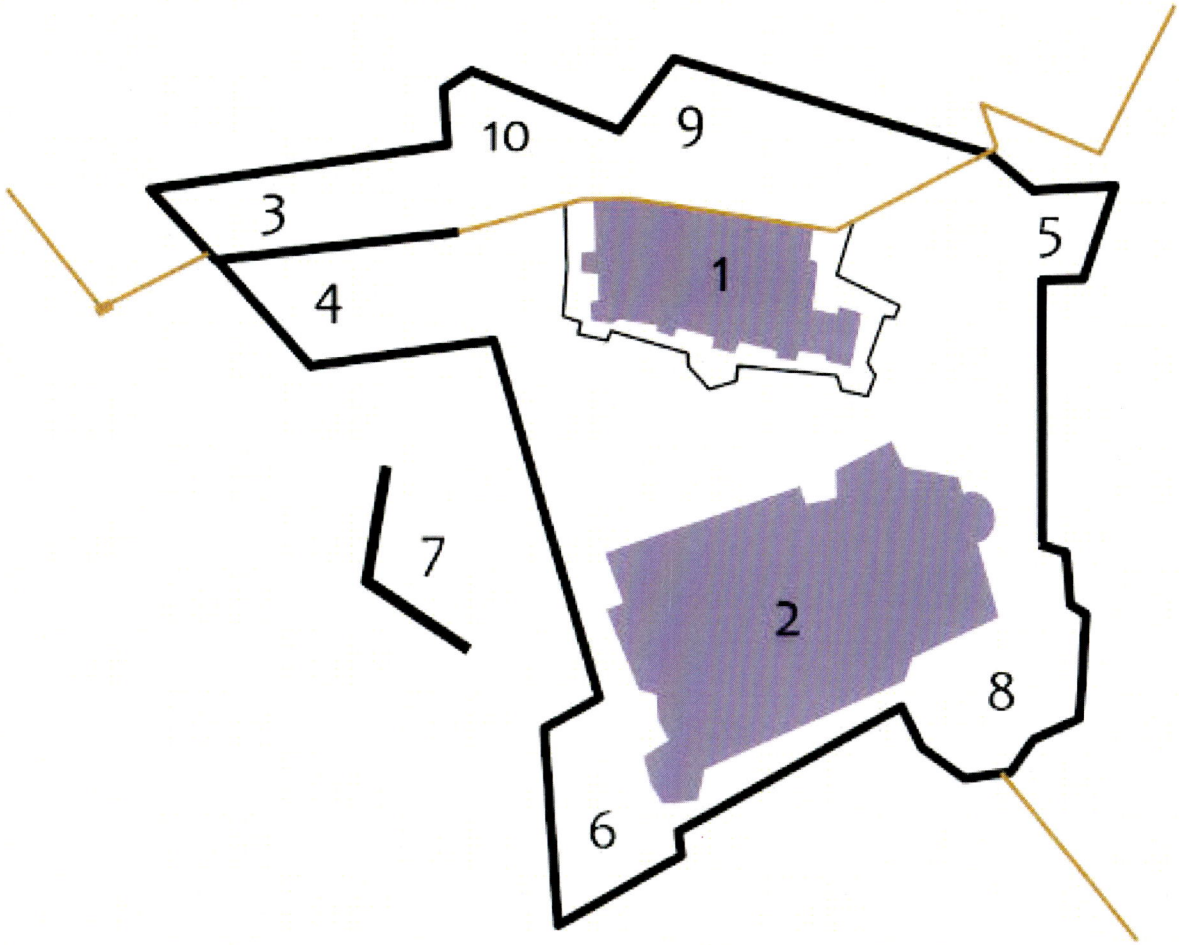

Map 2.2: Details of the fortress of Lleida from 1644 and 1648. Adapted from Burgueño (2001).

1. Castle of Lleida, called La Suda
2. Cathedral
3. Bastion of Puncegut
4. Bastion of the King
5. Bastion of Cantelmo
6. Bastion of the Assumption
7. Half-moon covering the entrance
8. Balcony of the Pilat
9. Bastion of the French
10. Bastion of the New Wall

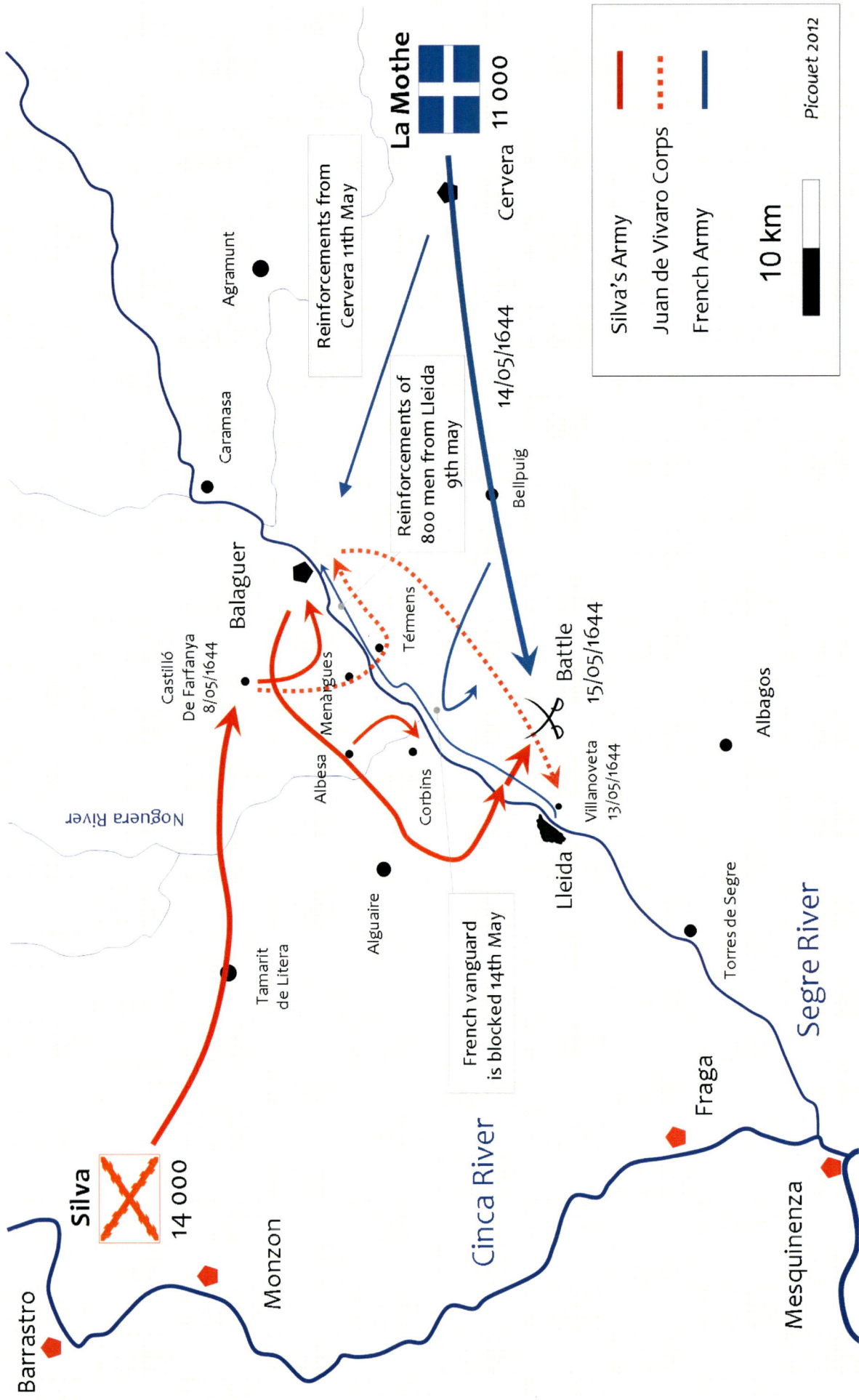

Map 3: Campaign of spring 1644, main movements of the Spanish and French troops.

Barrastro

Monzon

Cinca River

Mesquinenza

Fraga

Torres de Segre

Segre River

Albagos

Lleida

Villanoveta
13/05/1644

French vanguard
is blocked 14th May

Alguaire

Tamarit
de Litera

Noguera River

Albesa

Corbins

Menàrgues

Castilló
De Farfanya
8/05/1644

Balaguer

Térmens

Battle
15/05/1644

Reinforcements of
800 men from Lleida
9th may

Caramasa

Agramunt

Bellpuig

14/05/1644

Reinforcements from
Cervera 11th May

La Mothe

Cervera 11 000

Silva

14 000

Legend:

Silva's Army	
Juan de Vivaro Corps	
French Army	

Picouet 2012

10 km

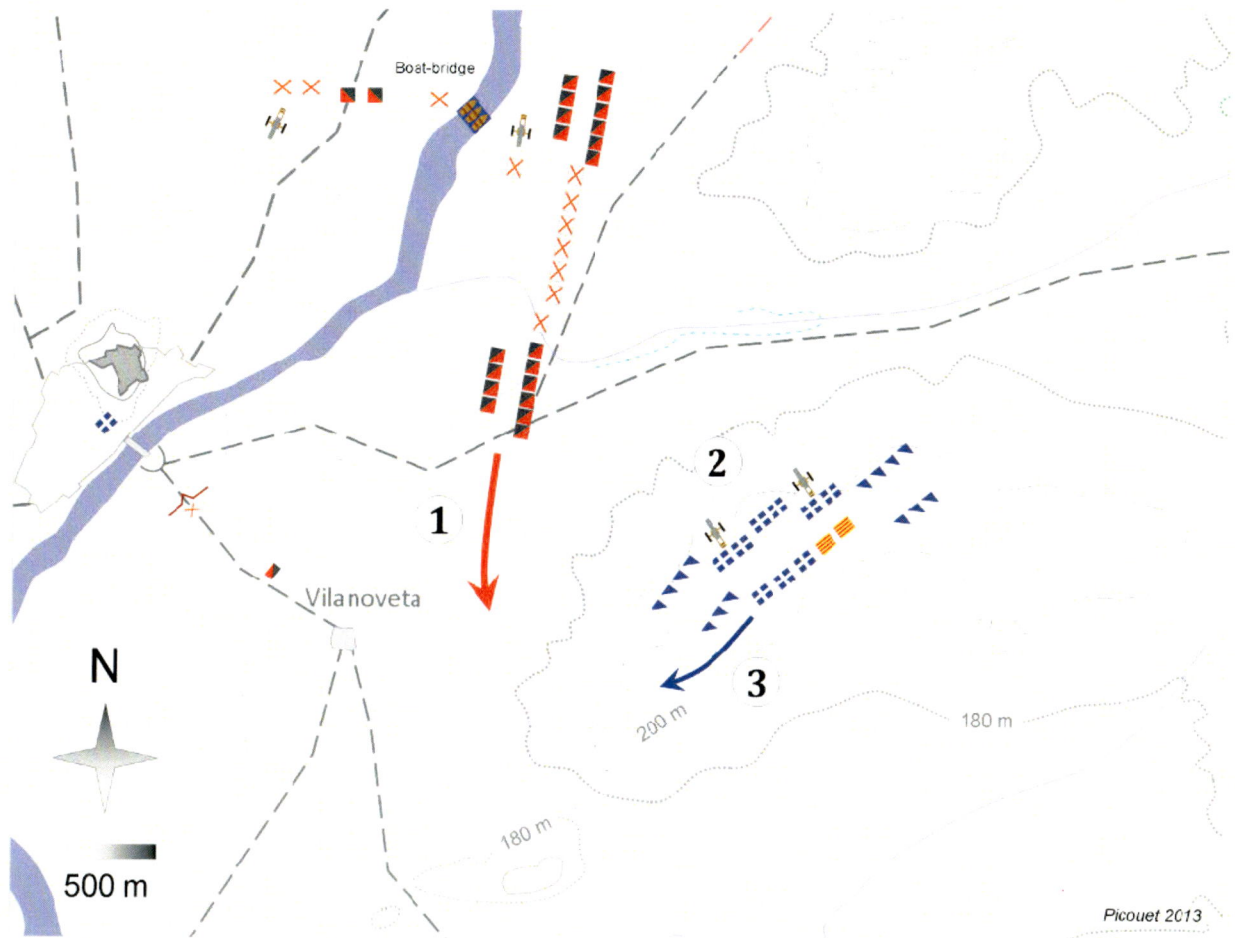

Map 4.1: Battle of Lleida, 15th May 1644 (Phase 1)

1. Initial movement of the Spanish army after crossing the river Segre.
2. French battery opens fire on the Spanish army, causing some casualties.
3. Thinking that their position could be outflanked, the French extend their front with the second line to occupy the entire hill.

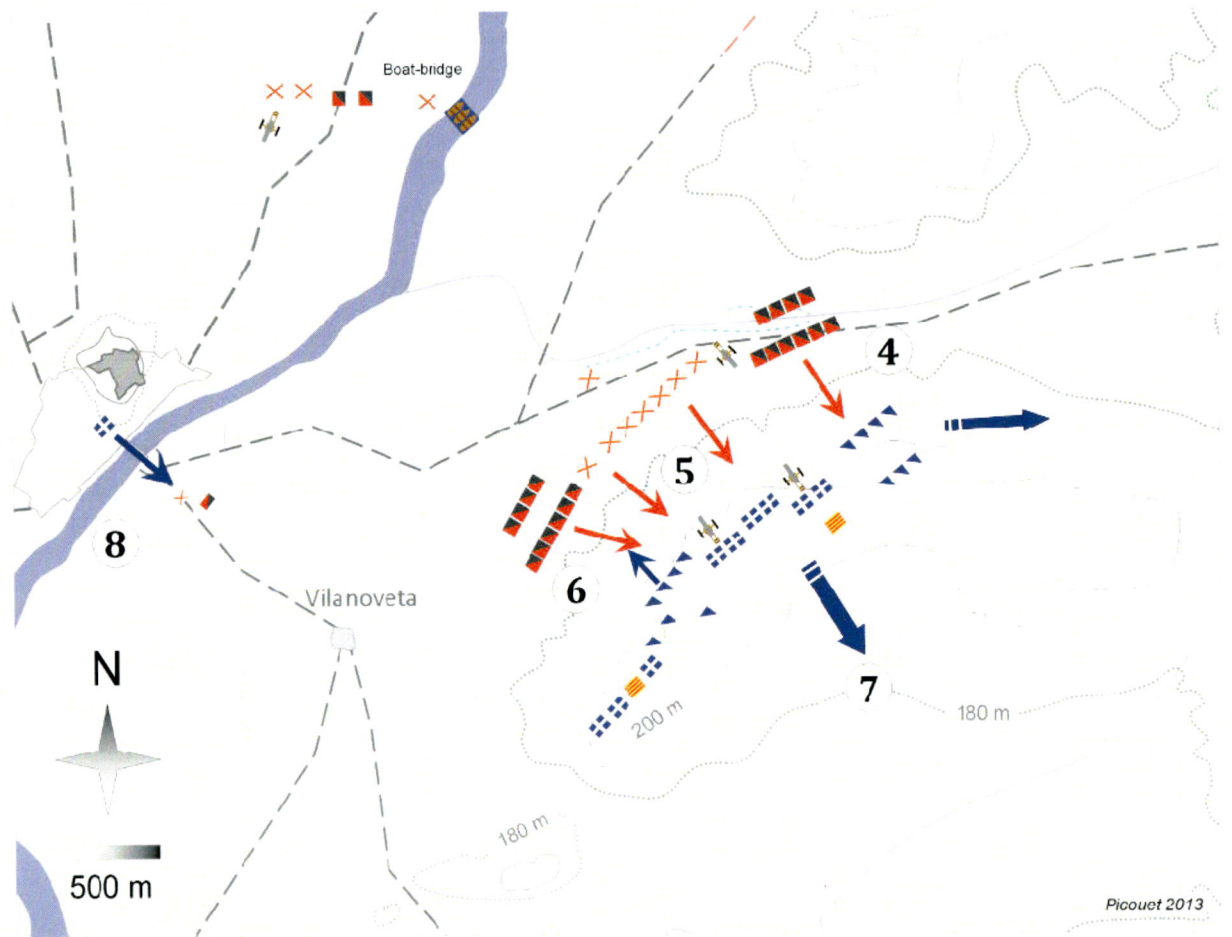

Map 4.2: Battle of Lleida, 15th May 1644 (Phase 2)

4. Successful advance of the Spanish cavalry of Cerralbo. Their French opponents put up little resistance before giving ground.
5. In the centre, each battalion of the Spanish infantry attacks its French counterpart. Despite artillery support, most of the French infantry offer little resistance. Only the Regiment of de la Mothe puts up a fight, with the Tercio of Mascareña on the right of the line.
6. On the right, the Spanish cavalry meets the incoming French squadrons. Their victory was secured when the Spanish commit a reserve of three squadrons from their second line.
7. The Spanish occupy the main part of the hill defeating the last resistance of the French. The Regiment of La Mothe is destroyed and the French commander loses the control of his army.
8. Meanwhile the garrison of Lleida manages to defeat those Spanish troops blocking the bridge of Lleida. The entrance to the city is open.

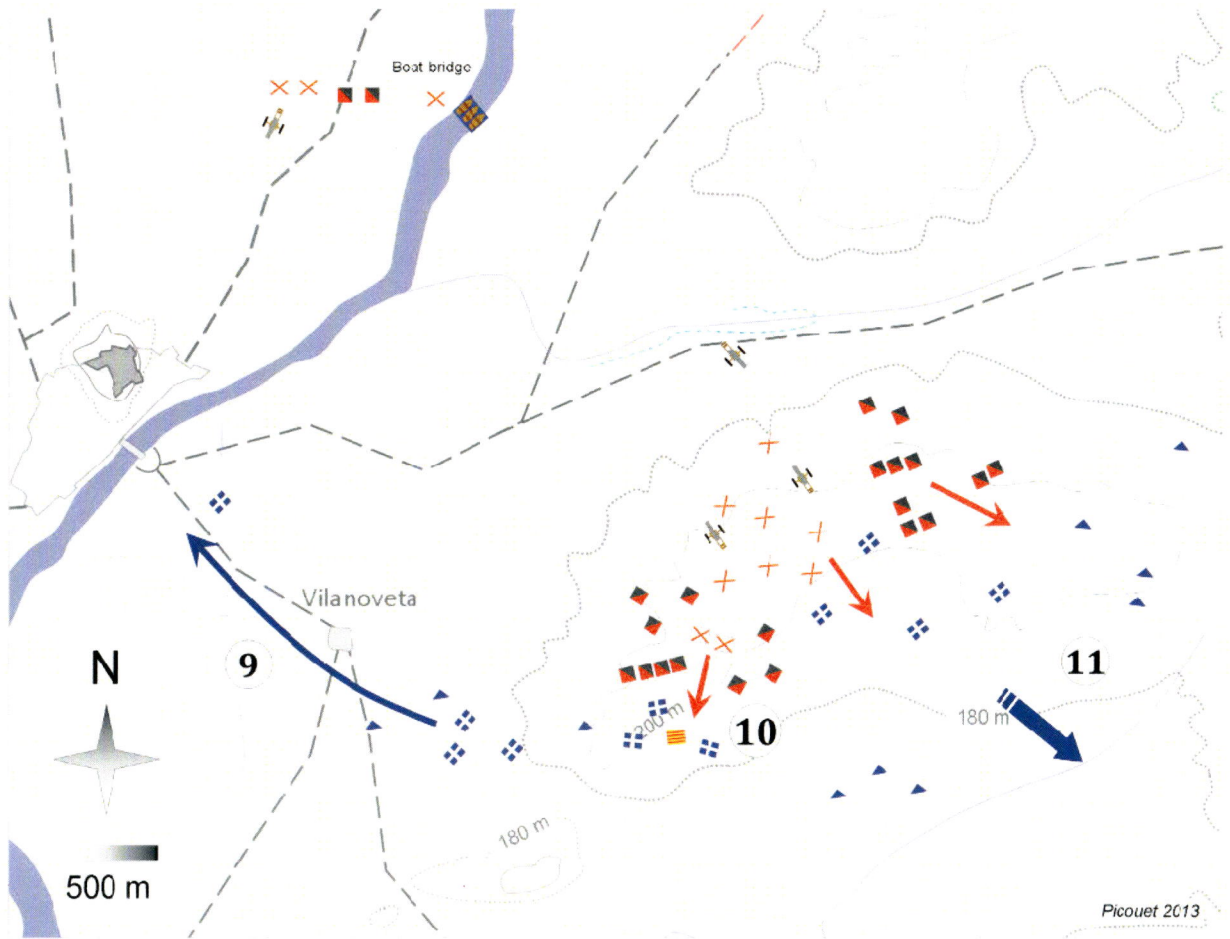

Map 4.3: Battle of Lleida, 15th May 1644 (Phase 3)

9. Following his orders, the Marquis of la Valière makes contact with the garrison of Lleida and leads a strong detachment of 2,000 men into the city.

10. Mortara sends Juan de Vivaro to pursue three French battalions. After a short resistance most of the French infantry surrender.

11. Finally, the Spanish occupy the entire hill while the French soldiers flee as fast as possible.

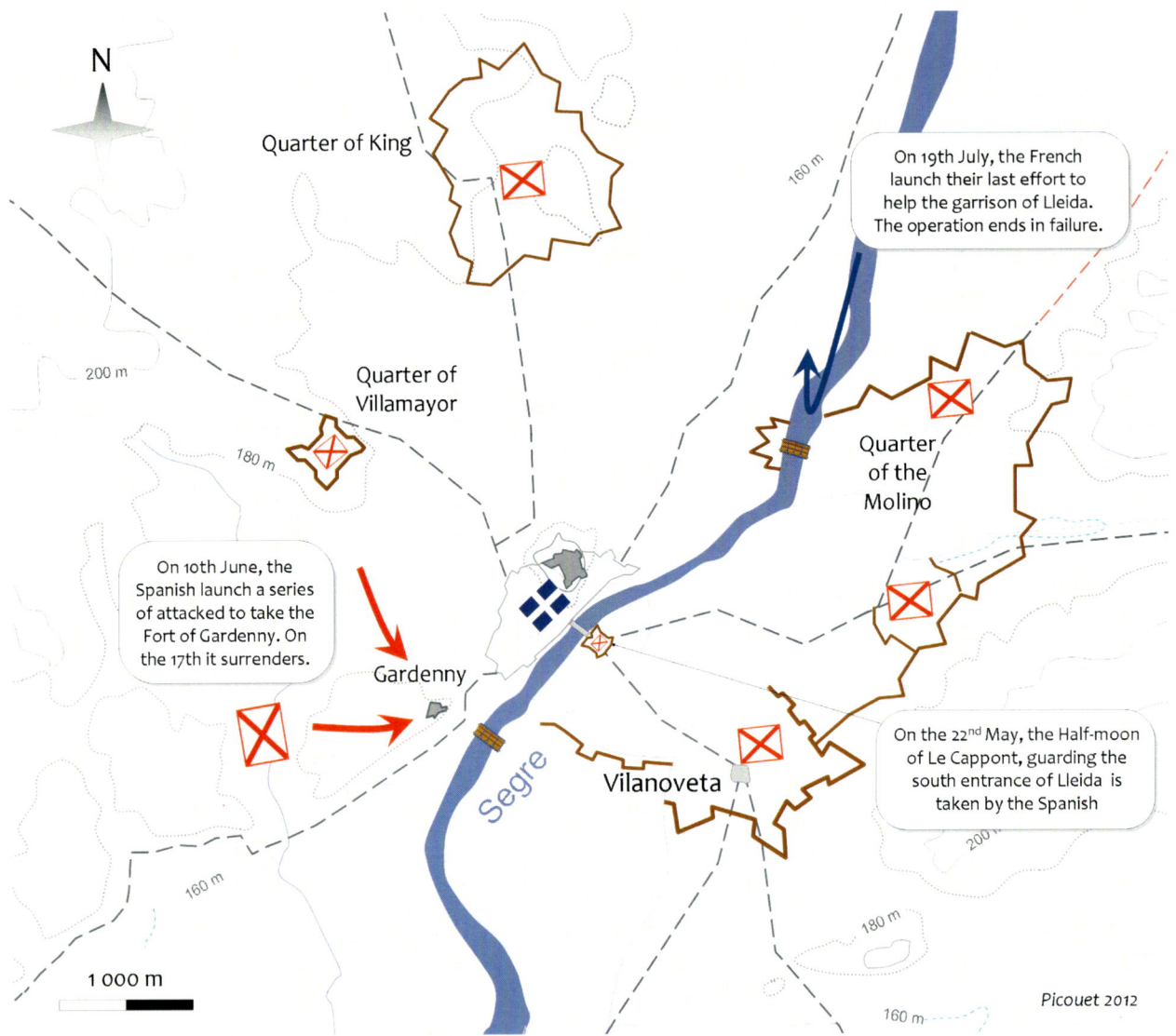

N

Quarter of King

On 19th July, the French launch their last effort to help the garrison of Lleida. The operation ends in failure.

160 m

200 m

Quarter of Villamayor

180 m

Quarter of the Molino

On 10th June, the Spanish launch a series of attacked to take the Fort of Gardenny. On the 17th it surrenders.

Gardenny

Segre

Vilanoveta

On the 22nd May, the Half-moon of Le Cappont, guarding the south entrance of Lleida is taken by the Spanish

200

180 m

160 m

1 000 m

Picouet 2012

Map 5: Sketch of the main positions of the Spanish army during the siege of Lleida from 13th May to 30th June 1644. Adapted from the document BNE Bellas Arte n.Inv. 68186.

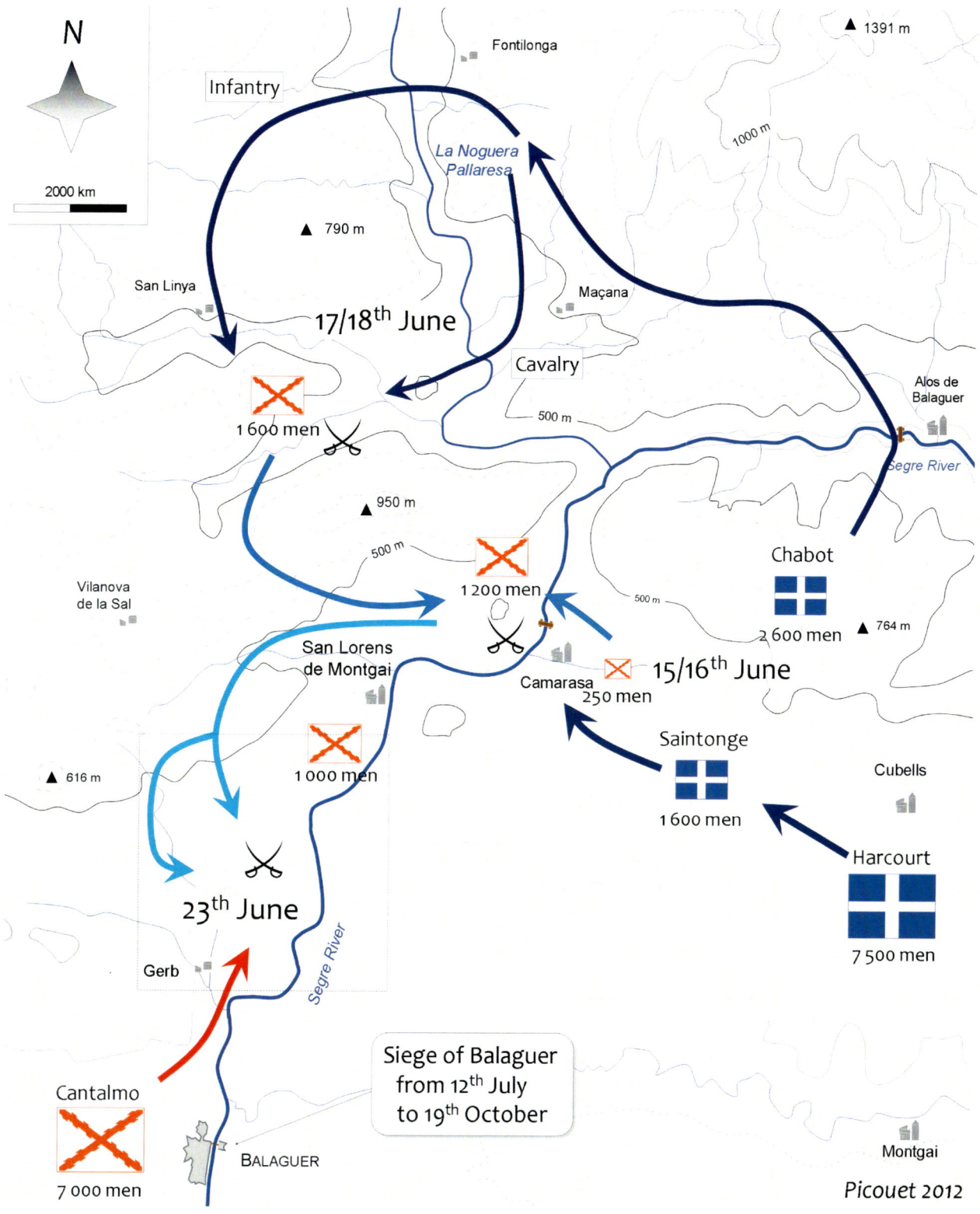

Map 6: Campaign of 1645, showing the main movements of the French and Spanish armies.

The following labels appear on the map:

N

2000 km

Fontilonga

▲ 1391 m

Infantry

La Noguera Pallaresa

1000 m

▲ 790 m

San Linya

Maçana

17/18ᵗʰ June

Cavalry

Alos de Balaguer

500 m

Segre River

1 600 men

▲ 950 m

500 m

Chabot

Vilanova de la Sal

1 200 men

2 600 men

▲ 764 m

San Lorens de Montgai

500 m

Camarasa

15/16ᵗʰ June

250 men

▲ 616 m

1 000 men

Saintonge

Cubells

1 600 men

Harcourt

23ᵗʰ June

7 500 men

Gerb

Segre River

Siege of Balaguer from 12ᵗʰ July to 19ᵗʰ October

Montgai

Cantalmo

BALAGUER

Picouet 2012

7 000 men

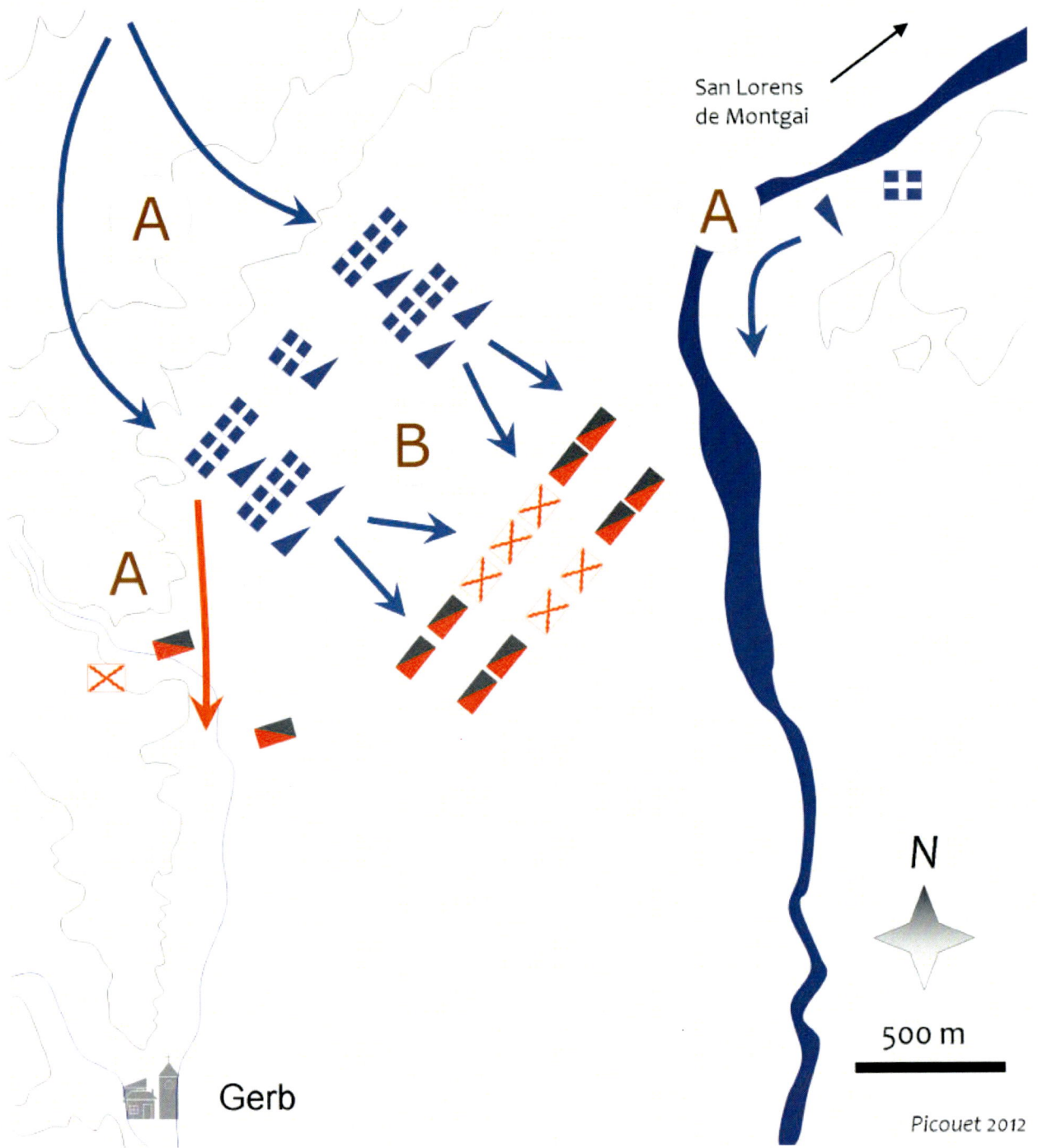

Map 7.1: The Battle of San Lorenz de Montgai, 23rd June 1645 (Phase 1)

A. Harcourt engages in a flanking movement across the hills surrounding San Lorenz of Montgai. He quickly manages to overwhelm the Spanish vanguard and deploys his army. At the same time, on the opposite side of the river Segre, a French detachment takes position to prevent the crossing of the river.

B. After deploying into two main blocks, the French launch a directly attack on the Spanish position, seizing a decisive advantage over their enemy.

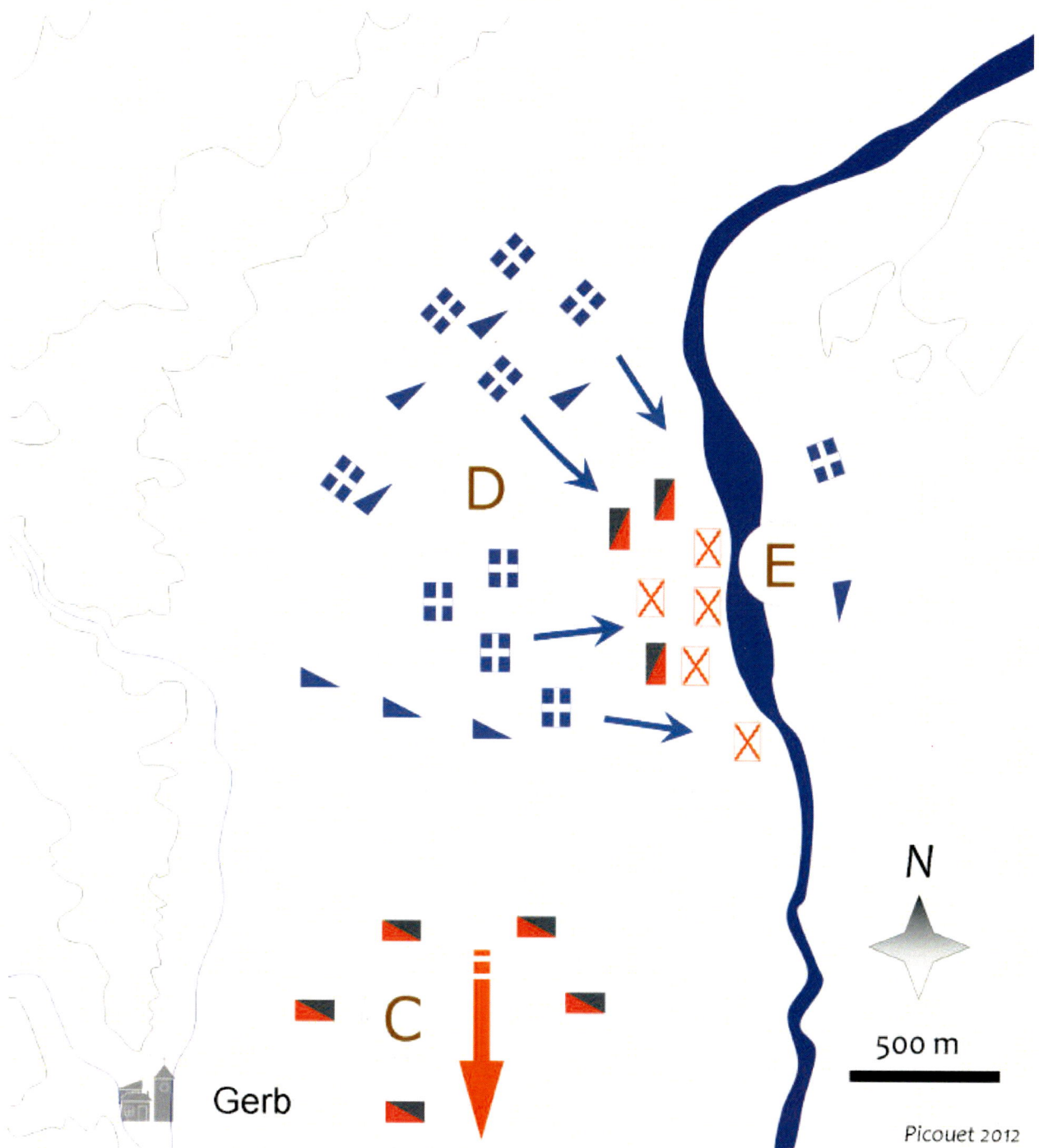

Map 7.2: The Battle of San Lorenz de Montgai, 23rd June 1645 (Phase 2)

C. The first force to break is the Spanish cavalry. After fierce fighting they withdraw to the city of Balaguer.

D. On the battlefield, despite hard fighting, the French manage to push back the Spanish infantry toward the river bank.

E. After hours of fighting, and surrounded by superior French forces, the Marquis of Mortara is obliged to surrender.

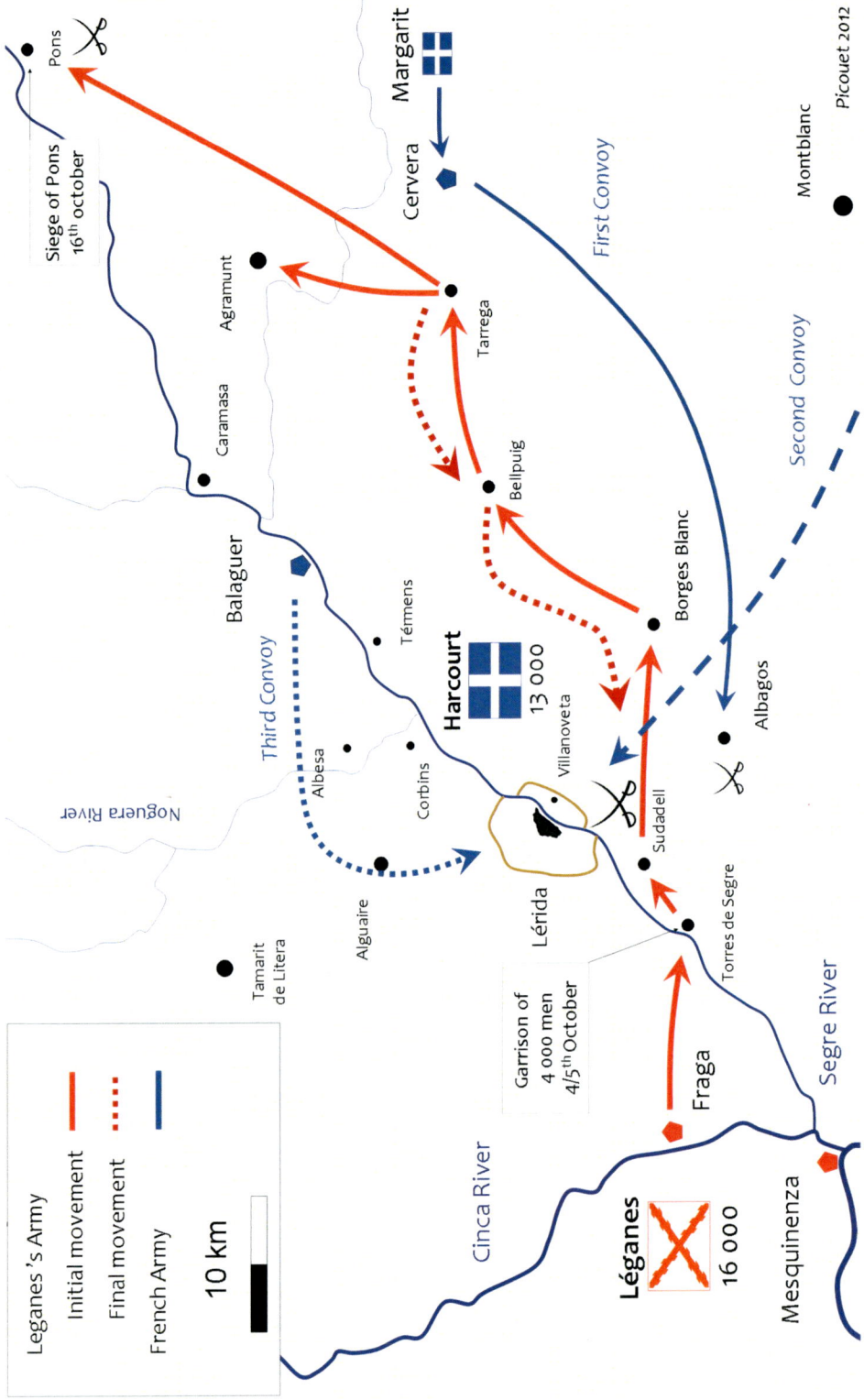

Map 8: Campaign of 1646, showing the movements of the Spanish army in the autumn and also of the French-Catalan convoys to supply Harcourt's forces.

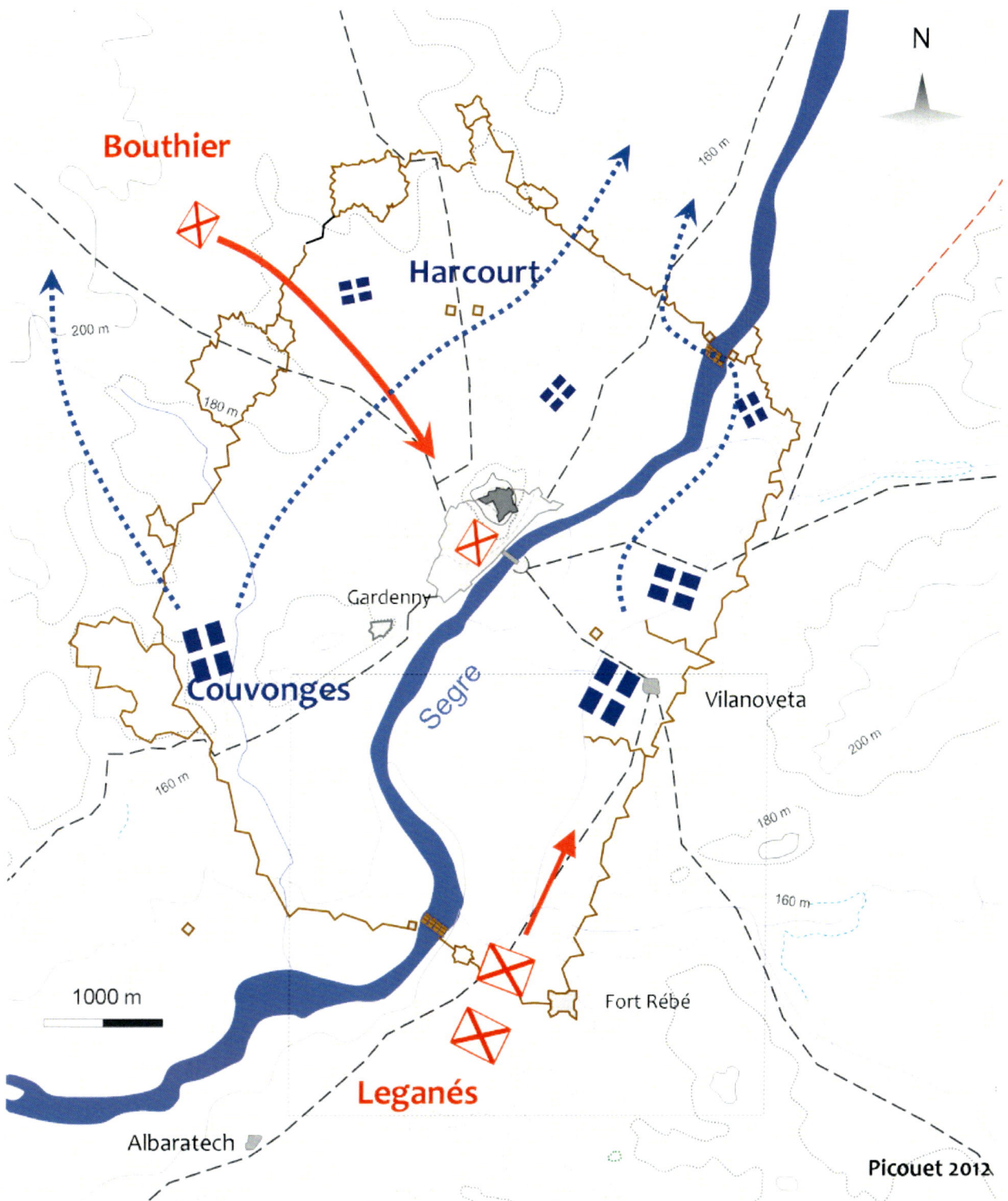

Map 9: Main positions of the French and Spanish forces around Lleida in November 1646. Red arrows indicate the movement of the Spanish and the blue dots show the retreat of the French. Adapted from H. Pannels BNE Seccion Manuscrito Ms 2377 (fol 185) 1646

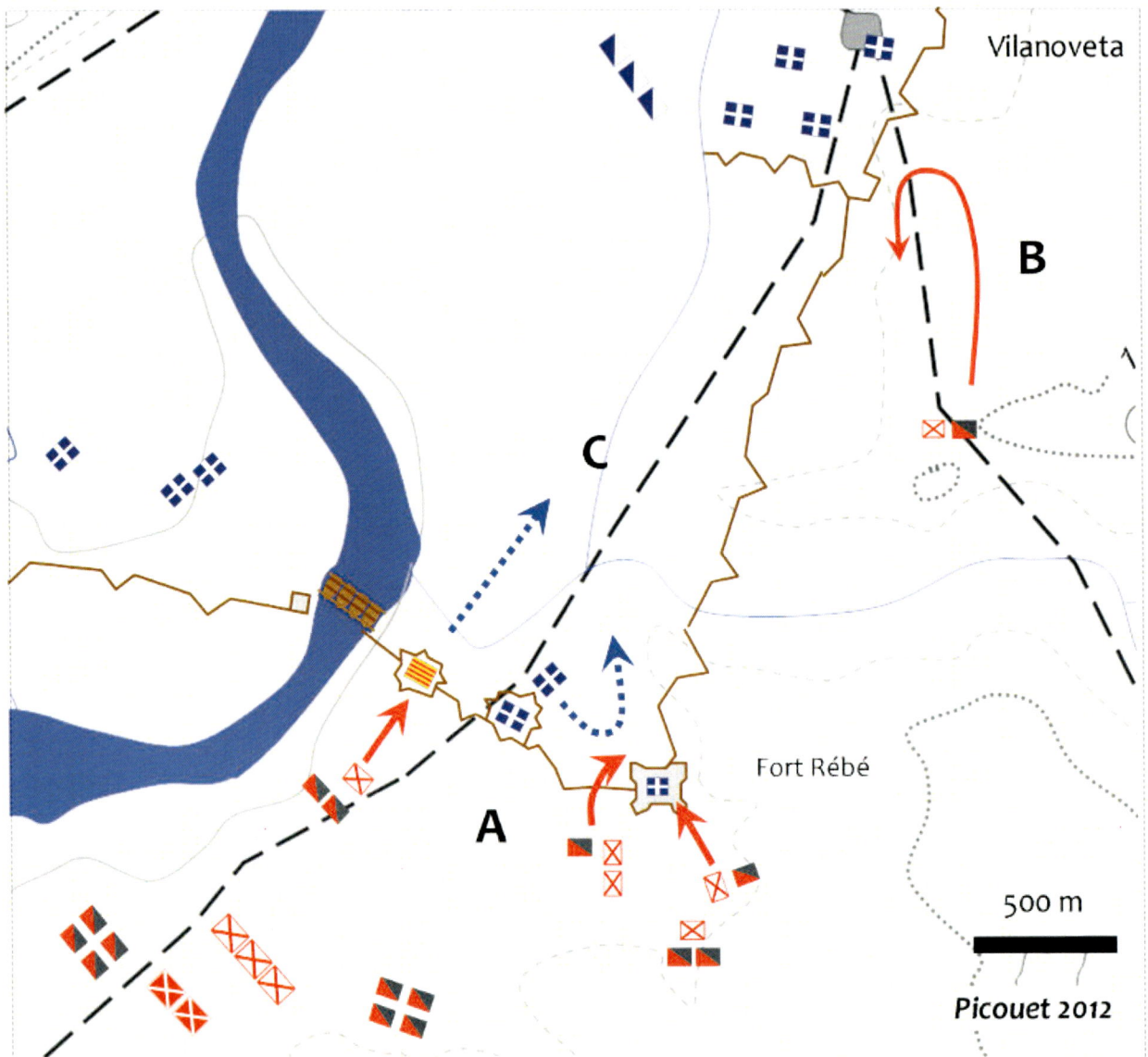

Map 10.1: The battle of Santa Cecilia, 21st–22nd November 1646 (Phase 1)

A. The attack on Fort Rébé starts at 10 p.m. with two columns. Despite the presence of three light guns the reduced garrison of 80 men is subdued in only 20 minutes. On the river bank, the Walloon battalion attacks the fortification occupied by the Catalans. After heavy fighting, in which several Catalan officers are killed, the defenders are expelled, fleeing to the rear in the direction of Vilanoveta.

B. In front of the quarter of Vilanoveta a small Spanish detachment of less than 300 men conducts a diversion. They manage to confuse the French commander for some crucial hours.

C. After the initial shock, the Count of Origny, colonel of the Regiment of Champagne, manages to organise a battalion and fights a bitter rearguard action against the Spanish. The Regiment of Champagne suffers heavy losses but wins some time for Harcourt. Contrary to orders, the Duke of Infantado leads his six cavalry squadrons in pursuit the enemy and Tuttavilla is obliged to support his action with two tercios.

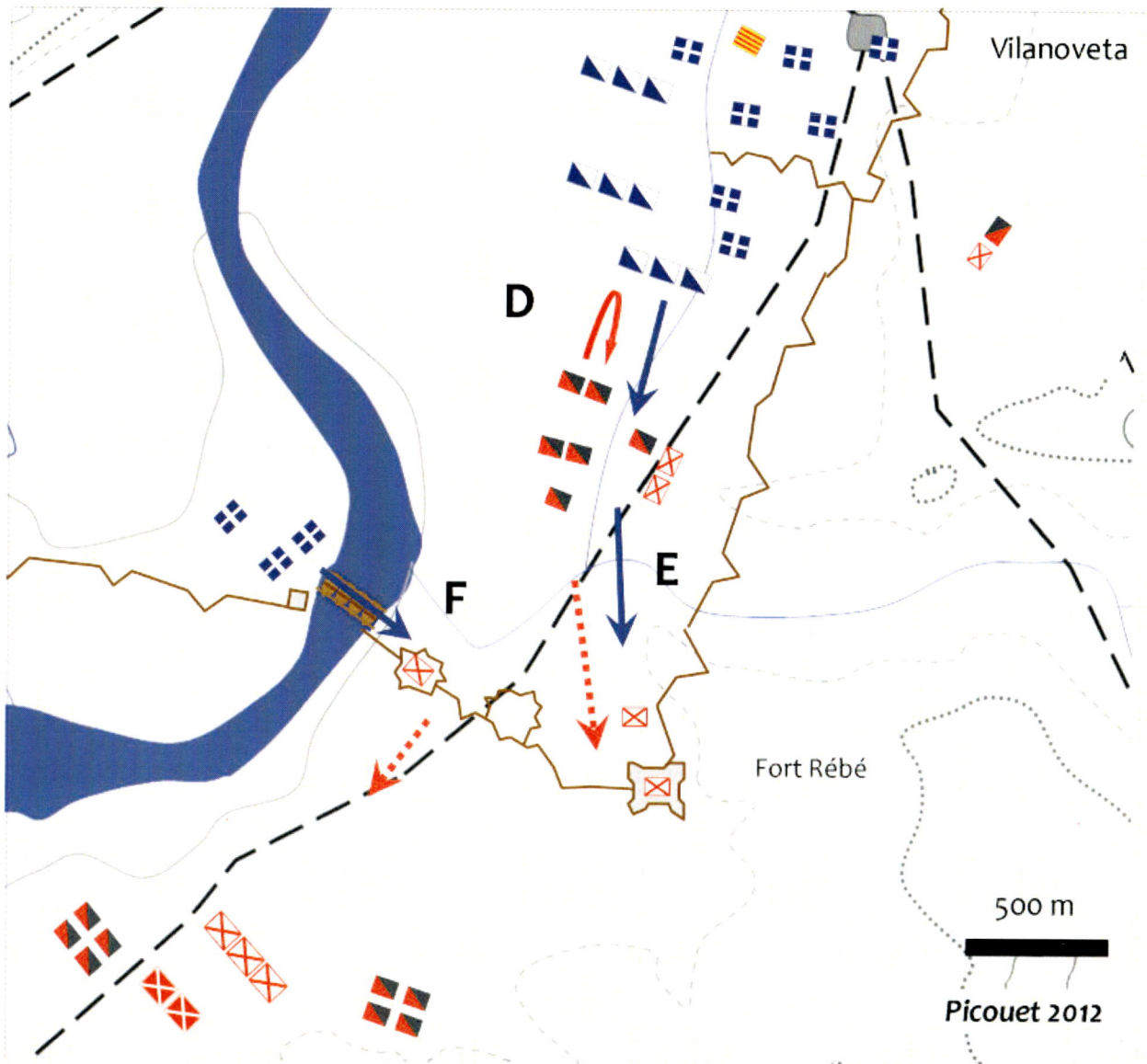

Map 10.2: The battle of Santa Cecilia, 21st–22nd November 1646 (Phase 2)

D. The Duke of Infantado meets the superior force of Harcourt, with 800 Horse and 1,000 Foot, just in front of Villanoveta. With the elite of his cavalry and the support of three to four infantry regiments, Harcourt engages and wins the struggle against the advancing Spanish. The Duke of Infantado's force withdraws in confusion towards Fort Rébé.

E. Seeing the arrival of disordered troops, Don Pablo de Parada organises the defence of Fort Rébé. When Harcourt arrive with his troops to retake the fort, he is met by heavy fire from the Spanish musketeers and is blocked by solid squadrons of pikemen.

F. The Count of Couvonges conducts a counterattack; he manages to cross the river Segre and to retake the Catalan fortifications. However he is unable go further because some reorganised squadrons of the Duke of Infantado are blocking the way.

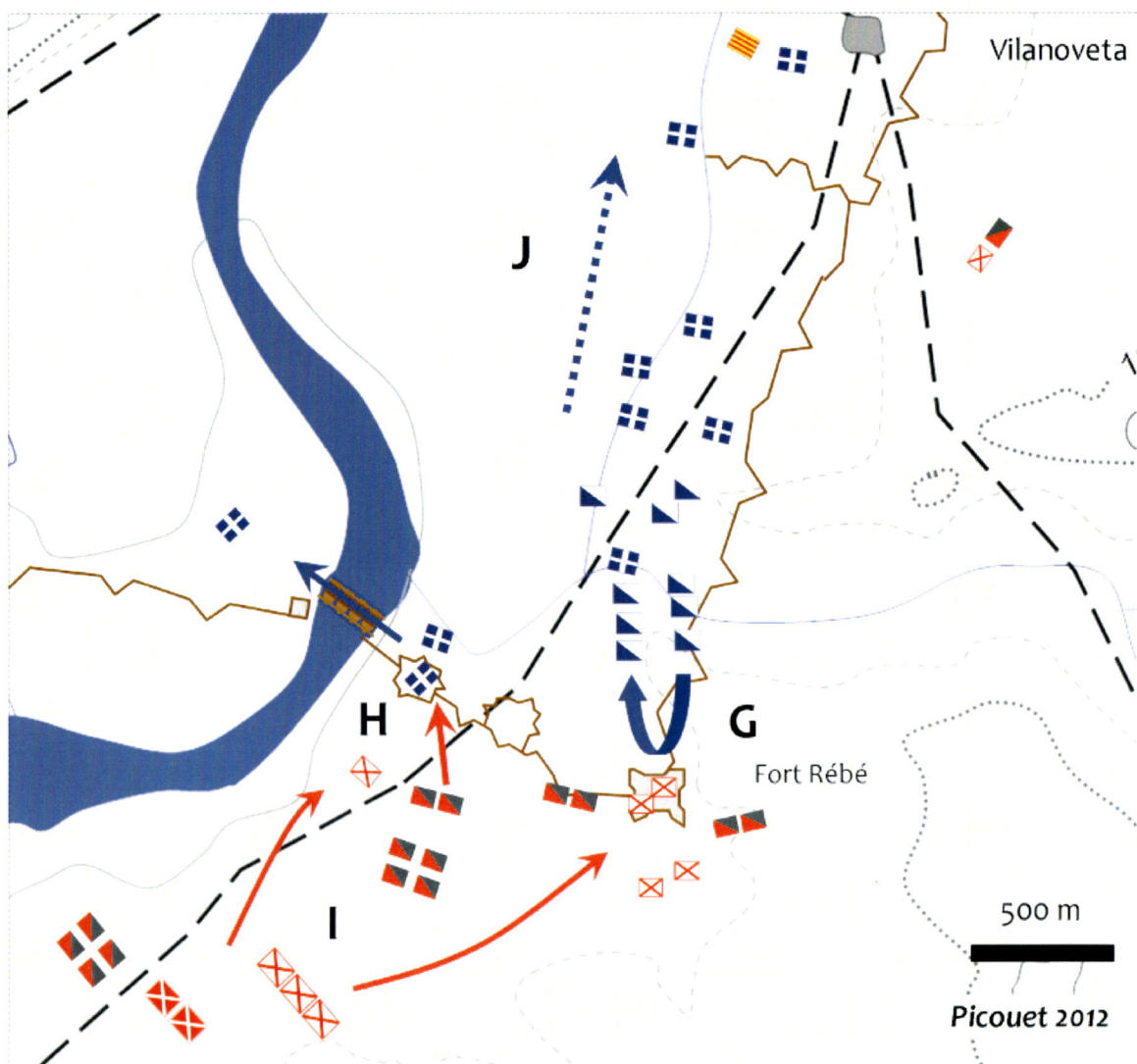

Map 10.3: The battle of Santa Cecilia, 21st–22nd November 1646 (Phase 3)

G. Leganes has only confused information of the battle; there is nothing from Bouthier, and the men fleeing the battlefield are shouting that the battle was lost. Fortunately he receives a message from Parada and Villamayor asking for reinforcements and orders several *mangas* from his tercios to be sent to Fort Rébé. Harcourt charges with all the troops he has to hand, but the frontage is too narrow and the Spanish have a good defensive position. Each French attack is met by fierce resistance and French troops suffer heavy casualties.

H. The cavalry of the Duke of Infantado, with the reorganised Walloon troops, attack Couvonges and manages to regain the fortification. The French have to retire to the other side of the river.

I. Harcourt is unable to retake the position and orders a retreat to Vilanoveta. At 5 a.m. news of the arrival of a Spanish force in Lleida was spreading all around the French position. The French have no information concerning the size of this force, they only understand that Spanish troops with Horse and Foot have arrived in Lleida and that they could threaten their withdrawal to Balaguer. Harcourt now has little control of his troops and a general panic spreads along the French who abandon all their guns and the baggage.

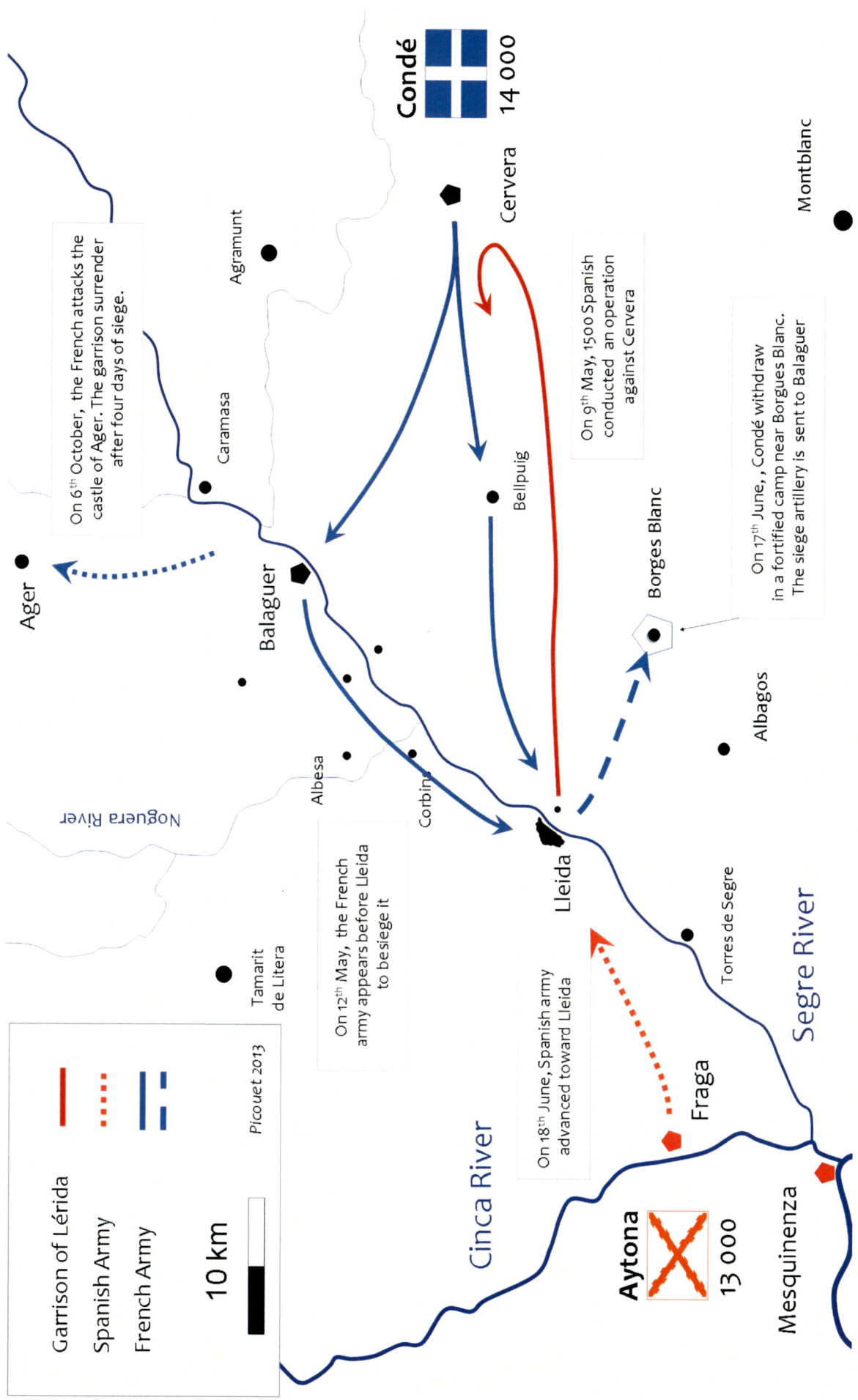

Map 11: Main movements of the 1647 campaign, before and after the siege.

Condé 14 000

On 6th October, the French attacks the castle of Ager. The garrison surrender after four days of siege.

On 9th May, 1500 Spanish conducted an operation against Cervera

On 17th June, , Condé withdraw in a fortified camp near Borgues Blanc. The siege artillery is sent to Balaguer

On 12th May, the French army appears before Lleida to besiege it

On 18th June, Spanish army advanced toward Lleida

Cervera

Agramunt

Caramasa

Bellpuig

Borges Blanc

Ager

Balaguer

Albesa

Corbins

Albagos

Montblanc

Noguera River

Tamarit de Litera

Lleida

Torres de Segre

Cinca River

Segre River

Fraga

Mesquinenza

Aytona 13 000

Legend:

Garrison of Lérida

Spanish Army

French Army

10 km

Picouet 2013

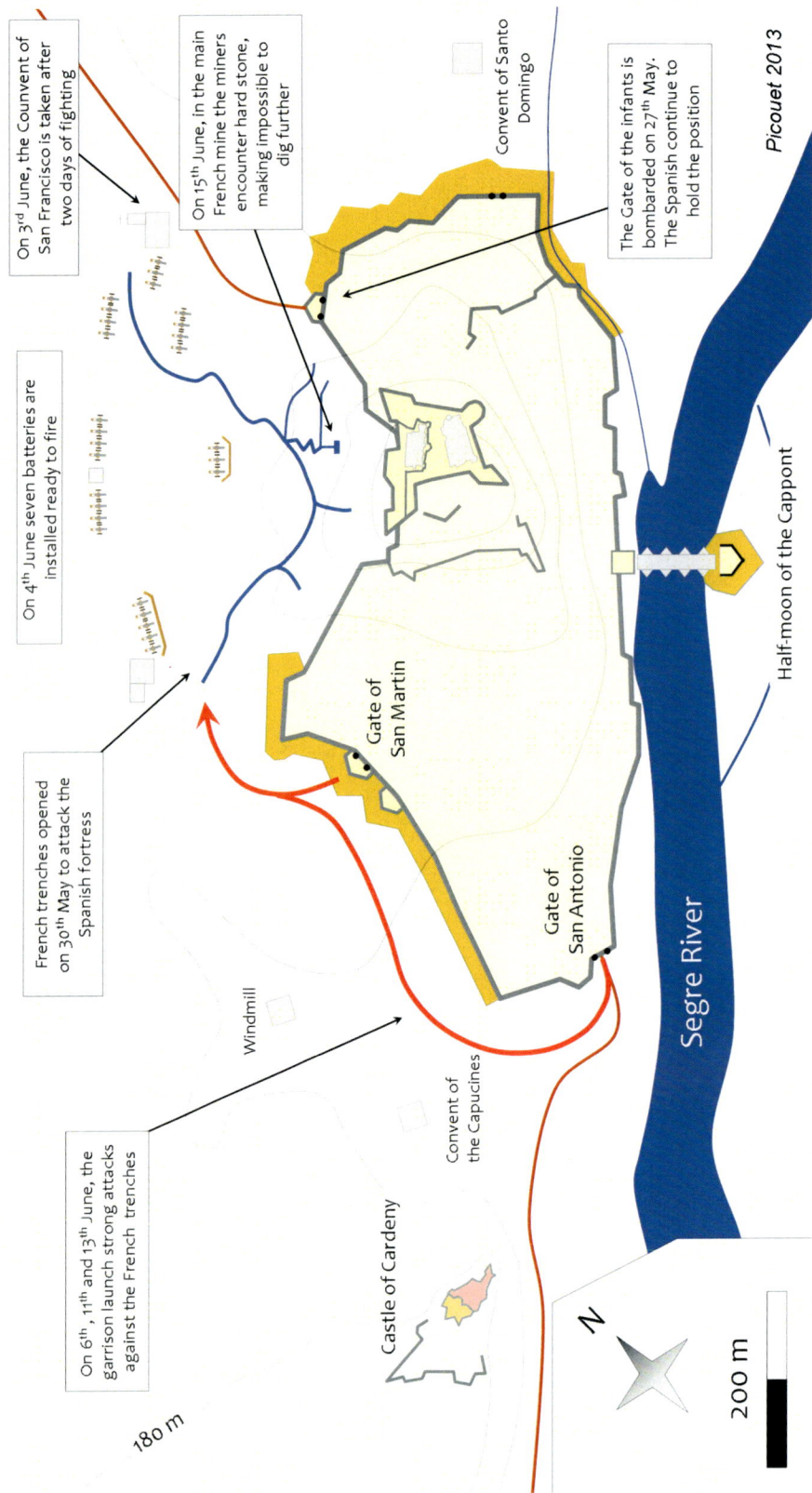

On 3rd June, the Couvent of San Francisco is taken after two days of fighting

On 15th June, in the main French mine the miners encounter hard stone, making impossible to dig further

On 4th June seven batteries are installed ready to fire

Convent of Santo Domingo

The Gate of the infants is bombarded on 27th May. The Spanish continue to hold the position

French trenches opened on 30th May to attack the Spanish fortress

Picouet 2013

On 6th, 11th and 13th June, the garrison launch strong attacks against the French trenches

Gate of San Martin

Half-moon of the Cappont

180 m

Windmill

Gate of San Antonio

Segre River

Convent of the Capucines

Castle of Cardeny

N

200 m

Map 12: Main operations during the siege of Lleida from 12th May to 17th June.

Chapter 1
The Strategic Situation on the
Catalan Front in 1640-1642

1.1 Political Situation

In 1624, Philip's Valido, the Count-Duke Olivares proposed a new program called the *Union de Armas* to create a reserve army of 140,000 men,[1] financed by all the components of the Spanish monarchy.[2] For the Council of State, the main idea of the *Union de Armas* was to reduce the dependency of the monarchy on Castilla and to share the burden of defence with the other provinces. The program contemplated not only the recruitment and finance of the men, but also the delivery of grain, horses and other supplies to maintain an army. The *Union de Armas* was welcome in most of the provinces but met with resistance in Aragon and Valencia, and opposition in Catalonia and Portugal. The Catalan Cort (i.e. parliament) viewed their share of the burden as being too large in comparison with their population, and also that the *Union de Armas* was against Catalan's own law for the defence of the territory, summarised in the *Princeps Namque*.[3] Over

the decade of the 1620s, relations between the king´s government and the Cort of Barcelona were plagued by misunderstanding and distrust. In 1635, the war with France implied that Catalonia was becoming an active front. In January 1637, the king of Spain called for the application of the *Princeps Namque* to help the royal army defend the Catalan border and bring the war into French territory. The Cort of Barcelona and the viceroy, Cardona, had different interpretations of the *Princeps Namque* and when a Spanish army of 12,000 infantry, 1,300 cavalry and 31 guns, under Don Juan de Cerbellón, was sent to besiege Leucate,[4] few Catalans were part of it. The whole operation, initiated at the end of August, ended in failure for Spanish arms when a French army of 10,200 infantry and 1,000 cavalry under Charles de Schomberg managed to breach Spanish lines on 28th September. Apart from the military failure, one of the main consequences was that distrust between the viceroy Cardona[5] and the Catalans increased. The Catalans were now obliged to accommodate a small royal army in their province.[6] In 1638, with

---

[1] Of the 140,000 men, one third could be used in the armies of his majesty, the king of Spain.

[2] In theory the distribution was made according to the population of each estate: Castillas and America 44,000 men; Aragon 10,000 men; Catalonia 16,000 men; Valencia 6,000 men; Portugal 16,000 men; Naples 16,000 men; Sicily 6,000 men; Milan 8,000 men; Flanders 12,000 men; Mediterranean and Oceanic Islands 6,000 men.

[3] The *Princeps Namque* was one of the laws of the Cort of Barcelona that regulated the use of military force by the Prince for the defence of the Principality of Catalonia. It was created in the 11th century and was still in use in the 17th century. For more see D.J. Kagay (2002): 'The National Defence Clause and the Emergence of the Catalan State: *Princeps Namque* Revisted', in *Crusaders, Condottieri, and Cannon: Medieval Warfare in Societies*

around the Mediterranean, edited by Donald J. Kagay & L.J. Andrew Villalon, pp57–101.

[4] Leucate, defended by Monsieur du Barry with 400 men, was a key fortress for the French for defending Narbonne and the Languedoc region.

[5] Enric III d'Aragó Folc de Cardona i Córdoba, viceroy of Catalonia from 1633 to 1638.

[6] In July 1638, the population of the town of Palafrugell rebelled against the billeting of 300 men from a Spanish tercio. The seeds of hate between the Catalans and soldiers of the royal army were becoming more apparent.

operations being at the other end of the Pyrenees, around Fuenterrabia,[7] the Catalan front remained quiet. The following year Richelieu decided to attack Catalan soil, particularly the fortress of Salces. On 3rd June, Charles of Schomberg and the Prince of Condé arrived in front of the fortress of Salces with an army of 16,000 men, which was defended by 600 men. In five weeks, the French managed to dig two mines under the main wall. The explosion of these mines and following assault convinced the Spanish governor to capitulate on 19th July. The small Spanish army of 8,000 men, reinforced by 2,500 Catalans, was too weak to challenge the French. The Catalans decided to strongly reinforce the royal army and in September 1639, the new viceroy, the Count of Santa Coloma,[8] had in hand a strong force of 13,000 Catalans and 12,500 men from the royal army. On 18th September the fortress of Salces, now in French hands and with a garrison of 2,500 men (Governor Monsieur d'Espenan), was surrounded by the Spanish army. For more than three months the French garrison resisted. The Spanish faced a full scale attack on 2nd November, during which they managed to repulse all French attempts to penetrate their lines of circumvallation. In the Spanish camp there had been significant losses, but these were mostly due to desertion and illness. At last, on 6th January 1640, the French garrison capitulated, but as the next months would show it was a pyrrhic victory for the Spanish. Olivares decided that the royal army of 9,000 men[9] under the command

of the Marques of Balbases should be maintained and billeted in the Principality of Catalonia, mainly in eastern Catalonia between Roussillon and Barcelona and in the camp of Tarragona. The Catalans protested that the province was not as rich as Olivares thought, that they had fulfilled their duty during the siege of Salces, and that they were capable of defending their own borders. In short, they did not want to pay for the billeting of the infantry of the royal army. Lack of money led to indiscipline in the troops and in the spring a number of incidents arose in cities, towns and villages where the tercios of the royal army were located. In April incidents between troops and the locals became more and more violent and Santa Coloma did nothing to stop the tragedy because, in order to please his superior, he did not want to advise Olivares of the dangers of his policies. The tragedy started on 3rd May when a column of Italian soldiers from the Tercio of Leonarde di Moles was trapped and attacked in the town of San Celoni, only few soldiers managed to escape unhurt. Throughout May, between the attacks on soldiers and their reprisals on houses and villages, Catalonia was in a state of insurrection. The final episode occurred on 7th June, when 300 of the 2,000 reapers present in Barcelona for Corpus Christie, marched to the palace of the viceroy. The situation degenerated rapidly and at the end of the day twenty civil servants of the king, including the viceroy Santa Colona, laid dead in the streets of the city. On news of the death of the viceroy, the main commander of the Spanish army tried to regroup their forces. Juan de Garay gathered some 7,000 men in Roussillon and in Rosas, while the rest fled to the territory north of Valencia, or to Aragon. With some difficulty the Consell de Cent[10] of Barcelona managed to restore some order in the province but refused to accept the actual authority of the king of Spain. The Catalans quickly entered negotiations with an

---

[7] At the beginning of July 1638, a strong French army of 18,000 men, commanded by the Prince of Condé and supported by a strong fleet, attacked the city of Fuenterrabia. Revenge for Leucate was obtained when a Spanish army of 16,000 men breached the French lines and the Prince of Condé had to withdraw to France.

[8] Dalmau de Queralt i de Codina, count of Santa Coloma de Queralt, viceroy of Catalonia from 1639 to 1640.

[9] In April 1640, the infantry consisted of six Spanish tercios (Tercio of Guardias del rey, Tercio of Justo de Mendoza, Tercio of the Count of Molina, Tercio of the Marques of Mortara, Tercio of the Count of Aguilar and Tercio of Diego Caballero), two Neapolitans tercios (Tercio of Leonardo di Moles and Tercio of Jerónimo de Tuttavilla), the Wallon tercio of Molinguen, the Irish tercio of Tyrconnell, and the

---

regiment of the Duke of Modena. In total 164 companies (11 units), 1,479 officers and 6,699 soldiers.

10 The Consell de Cent was a governmental institution of the city of Barcelona. In 1640 it was lead by Francesc of Tamarit i de Rifà.

emissary of the king of France and by the treaty of Cervet (7th September) Catalonia would become a republic under the protection of the king of France. Richelieu now had his revenge; he had a foothold in the heart of the Spanish monarchy. Relations between the Catalans and Olivares were now broken beyond repair and the Spanish decided to send an army to take Barcelona as quickly as possible; the war of the reapers (*Guerra dels Segadors*) had begun. This conflict would be immersed into the global European confrontation and it would last until 1659, with the Peace of the Pyrenees.

1.2 Military Situation

Seeing that negotiations between Madrid and Barcelona were going nowhere, both the Spanish government and the Catalans prepared for war. In Madrid the Council of State ordered that the Army of Roussillon, some 7,500 men under Juan de Garay, was to block the French from the north and that the army of Marques of Le Velez would be assembled to the north of Valencia to march on Barcelona. In October 1640, the citizens of Tortosa seized power and handed over the city to Spanish troops. The Marques of Le Velez now had a bridge to safely cross the river Segre. On 25th October, the main Spanish army was in Tortosa waiting for the artillery train. By November 1640, the Spanish had a small army commanded by Nochera to protect Aragon, Juan de Garay was in Roussillon, and the Marques of Le Velez had 27,000 men in Tortosa. To oppose them the Catalans tried to organise a credible force with all the troops available (Somatem, the Militia of Barcelona, and private initiatives), but by that date they had less than 12,000 men in total and most of them new recruits with little or no military training. The French had some 1,400 men already present in Catalonia, with the regiments of Espenan and Serignan and some cavalry companies. On 6th December, the Army of Le Velez began the march to Barce-

lona with 23,000 infantry,[11] 3,100 cavalry and an artillery train of 24 guns. At first the army encountered some resistance at the pass of Balaguer, and later in the town of Cambrils, defended by 2,000–3,000 Catalans. Operations commenced on 8th December and five days later the garrison surrendered after an honourable resistance. Unfortunately atrocities[12] followed the surrender as part of the garrison was massacred, the leaders hung, and the city sacked. From this the Catalans understood that no mercy would be shown and that the war was to be total. The Spanish army continued its advance and on 24th December the important city of Tarragona was taken without a fight. Here the army received some supply from the armada and continued their march to Barcelona. On 23rd January the Catalan army,[13] supported by French forces, tried to block the Spanish at Martorell, but they were dispersed and most of them had to retire to Barcelona while the city was sacked by the victorious soldiers. When the Spanish army arrived in front of Barcelona, the Marquis of Le Vélez had only 15,000 foot and 2,000 horse; the rest were in garrisons or lost through battlefield casual-

---

[11] Infantry: four old tercios (Coronelia of the Guardias del rey, Tercio of Portugal, Tercio of Diego de Toledo and Tercio of Fernando de Tejada), three new tercios raised with conscripts (Tercio of Martin de los Arcos, Tercio of Pedro Lesaca and Tercio of Alonso Calatayud), two provincial tercios (Tercio of Castilla and Tercio Guipúzcoa), seven new Spanish regiments raised by nobles of Castilla (Regiments of the los Vélez, the Duke of Medinaceli, the Duke of Infantado, the Gran Prior of Castilla, the Marques of Morata, the Duke of Pastrana and the Count of Oropesa), the Walloon tercio of the Baron of Isenghien, the new Portuguese Tercio of Mascareña and the Irish Tercio of Hugh, Earl of Tyrone. The cavalry came from the companies of guards and two strong corps, the cavalry of the military orders under the command of Álvaro de Quiñones and the Royal Cavalry or *caballería ligera*, under the command of Carlo Maria Caracciolo.
[12] Following Ribas {2012}, the massacres started when Spanish soldiers tried to rob the defeated Catalans. The Spanish escort thought that the Catalans were trying to escape and opened fire, in less than 20 minutes 700 Catalans lay dead.
[13] In Martorell, the Catalan army had five regular tercios of infantry, a tercio of 700 light infantry called Miquelets, 300 cavalry and 6 light guns. They were supported by the French infantry regiment of Serignan and 300 French cavalry, in total 8,000 foot and 600 horse.

ties, sickness and desertion. The army was divided into three: on the right a strong force of 9,000 infantry under the Marquis of Torrecuso was to attack the Castle of Montjuich; on the left a force of 5,000 infantry and 1,700 cavalry under Juan de Garay was to cover the city gates; finally there was a reserve of 1,300 men in the Hospitalet de Llobregat. From the little information available on the action, Torrecuso's plan appears to have been to send a first wave on the right to test the defences, followed by a second wave to take them. The defence of Barcelona[14] was divided into the position of Montjuich, heavily fortified by the Catalans with the help of French officers, and the city of Barcelona proper. On the morning of 26th January 1641, the Spanish attack started with the advance of two columns of 1,000 men to occupy the hill of Monjuich. At first everything went according to plan, but the Spanish came in for a nasty surprise when they encountered the newly constructed trenches. The right column was stopped totally, losing many men, while the left column managed to take the trenches but was stopped when targeted by the artillery of the Castle. The second wave was also divided into two brigades, on the right the Spanish finally managed to force the first Catalan line, while on the left a first assault was launched with little success. When the right-hand column arrived in front of the Castle, Torrecuso ordered a full-scale attack, but the Spanish soldiers met with heavy fire from muskets and artillery guns and were repulsed with heavy losses. In front of Barcelona the Spanish cavalry, supported by musketeers, had taken up a position to block any movement from the city to the hill of Montjuich and the French decided to take the

initiative to remove this threat. At first the Spanish managed to block the French counterattack, but with the support of the artillery of the city, the Spanish had to withdraw to a safer position; communication between Barcelona and Monjuich was now possible. On the hill the situation was not good for the Spanish, the defence was stronger than expected and the Catalans managed to repulse all attacks against the Castle. Aware that the city would send reinforcements, Torrecuso launched a last assault at 3 p.m., but the exhausted Franco-Catalans managed to resist and the arrival of reinforcements from Barcelona stopped the attack. At 4 p.m., with a reinforcement of 2,000 men, the Franco-Catalans started to attack the Spanish. The decimated Spanish units stood at first but rapidly withdrew from the hill and panic spread among the soldiers. The Spanish commander decided to call off the attack and withdrew his army to the village of Sants, a few kilometres from Barcelona. Next day the Spanish council of war acknowledged that the demoralised Spanish forces could not renew the attack and on the news that French and Catalan reinforcement were going to Barcelona, the Spanish undertook a difficult retreat to Tarragona. During the Battle of Montjuich they had lost close to 4,000 men, including dead and wounded and 19 flags; Catalans losses were probably less than 200 men.

The terrific battle of Monjuich was followed by an offensive against Tarragona in May 1641, with the new French army of Philippe de la Mothe-Houdancourt consisting of 12,000 French supported by 3,000 Catalans and the French fleet of Soudis (26 vessels, 4 fire ships and 19 galleys). The Spanish resisted stoutly with the army of Le Velez. Over a period of four months the two armies fought each other on the plain around Tarragona, while at sea the French and Spanish fleets fought two major battles. On 20th August the Spanish fleet of 30 ships and 29 galleys forced the French blockade and escorted 65 transport ships, full of supplies, into the city. Five days later, Sourdis was forced to retire to Marseille and Toulon, the offensive against Tarragona was over. In Roussillon, since June 1641, the French had

---

14 On the hill of Monjuich there were seven Catalan companies guarding the newly dug trenches and four companies in the castle of Monjuich with eight guns. The defenders were supported by 300 French from the regiment of Servignan, distributed amoungst the Catalan companies to reinforce their efficiency. In Barcelona there was a strong Catalan force consisting of four tercios from the Coronelia of Barcelona, four companies of cavalry, and a French detachment composed of the rest of the regiment of Servignan, the regiment of Espenan and five French cavalry squadrons.

been skirmishing with Spanish forces in Perpignan, Collioure, Salces and Rosas further to the south. The following year, Richelieu and the French government sent substantial numbers of troops with the objective of seizing control of the province of Roussillon.[15] The elite of the French army (15,000 foot and 4,000 horse) was deployed in this operation and even the French King, Louis XIII, came to Narbonne to follow the actions. At the beginning of the year, the Count-Duke Olivares ordered supplies and reinforcements to be sent to the garrisons of Roussillon in preparation for the French offensive. In January the two sides fought over each convoy that moved from Collioure to Perpignan. In March 1642 the Spanish had probably 8,000-9,000 men distributed as follows: 3,000 men in Perpignan, 2,500 men in Collioure, 500 men in Salces and the rest in Rosas. On 13th March 10,000 French under the command of the Marshal de la Meilleraye and supported by the fleet of Sourdis laid siege on Collioure, while the rest of the French army surrounded Perpignan. For three weeks, daily engagements took place on the hills surrounding the fortress as well as assaults on the walls of Collioure. At last, on 9th April, the French ignited a mine under a tower, destroying a section of the wall. Two days later the Spanish commander, the Marques of Mortara, surrendered. Now Perpignan was completely surrounded and it was only a matter of time before the city would surrender due to a lack of supplies. Meantime, the Spanish council of war sent an order to Pedro Antonio de Aragon, Marques of Probar, to reinforce the forces of Roussillon by crossing Catalan territory from Tarragona to Rosas. With a picked force of 2,000 horse and 1,000 musketeers on horse, Pedro

Antonio de Aragon set out on 24th March from Tarragona. Unfortunately for the Spanish noblemen, the French and Catalans were full alerted and on 28th March, the Spanish fought a decisive battle near Granollers, where they lost 1,000 men, dead, wounded or prisoners. Pedro de Aragon attempted to withdraw to Tarragona, but on 30th March he was surrounded by 8,000 French and Catalans near Vilafranca del Penedes and had to surrender to avoid the futile massacre of his men.

As we have seen, in Perpignan, the elite of the French army was closing all possible supply routes into the city. A little fighting took place between the garrison and French forces, but the final issue was in no doubt. The Spanish made an attempt to supply Roussillon, sending a powerful fleet,[16] but they were met by the French fleet based in Barcelona. From 30th June to 2nd July, the two fleets fought bravely, but with the loss of three galleons to one French ship of the line, the Spanish admiral had to withdraw to the Baleares Islands and the fate of Perpignan was sealed. On 9th September the city of Perpignan capitulated and the 500 survivors were repatriated to Spain after a long journey to reach the Spanish border at Fuenterrabia on the west coast.

After the misfortune of Pedro de Aragon, Spanish forces in Tarragona undertook a small offensive operation, capturing the town of el Vendrell on 30th March. After this action, the Spanish army remained inactive, probably because they were expecting reinforcements. On the French side, de la Mothe-Houdancourt took the initiative in May, capturing several villages and towns of the County of the Ribargorça (Tamarit de Litera, Binefar and Montsó), north of Lleida. Operations ceased in Roussillon in September 1642; the substantial troops and supplies sent to Tarragona and Fraga by Count-Duke Olivares had remained inactive. Finally, on

---

15 From a maritime point of view, the French Atlantic squadron (Squadron of Ponant), under the command of Armand de Brézé, was sent to the Mediterranean in April 1642. In May 1642, the French fleet, under the overall command of Armand de Brézé, consisted in the Squadron of Ponant (21 vessels of the line, 6 fire ships and 2 smaller ships), the Squadron of Levant (19 vessels of the line, 6 fire ships and 4 smaller ships) and the 8 galleys of the Mediterranean. In total 64 ships to cover and establish superiority over the Catalan coast. In June, the fleet was in Barcelona.

16 Following C. de la Roncière [*Histoire de la Marine Française*, tome 2, Paris 1920] the Spanish fleet was under the command of Juan Alonso Idiáquez, Marques of Ciuedad Real, with 36 galleons/ships of the line, 10 galleys, 3 frigates, 3 patches, 6 fire ships, 6 tartanes and 35 long boats.

21st September, the 12,000 infantry and 4,000 cavalry of the Army of Tarragona began moving. The plan was to join with the Army of Fraga at Lleida and to try to capture the city. In Lleida, the French governor was trying, with some difficulty, to reinforce the old medieval walls and to construct a new fortress. With the reinforcement from the army in Roussillon, de la Mothe-Houdancourt also moved, following the Spanish Army of Tarragona on a parallel route. On 26th September, the Spanish arrived in les Borgues Blanques and two days later they were in Vilanoveta, south of Lleida. Here the Spanish commander discovered that the Army of Fraga had not arrived; with a lack of supply they turned west in the direction of Torres de la Segre. On 5th October, the Marques of Léganes joined the Army of Tarragona with 8,000 men of the Army of Fraga. Two days later, on 7th October, the whole army, estimated at 15,000 infantry, 5,000 cavalry and 9 guns, marched towards Vilanoveta to find the French army (9,000 infantry, 4,000 cavalry and 8 guns) deployed on a hill near the small town. Throughout the day the Spanish attacked the French position, but poor coordination and the performance of the French cavalry frustrated Spanish efforts. With night coming, Léganes was obliged to order a withdrawal to Torres de Segres. In the battle[17] the Spanish had lost between 1,500 and 2,000 men dead, wounded and prisoners, compared to 500 men for the French. The disaster was enhanced by heavy rains two days later; the Spanish were forced to cross the Segre rapidly, losing hundreds of men in the process. With a lack of supply, a high desertion rate, and the appearance of disease, Léganes had to disband the army. On the Catalan front the year of 1642 had ended in failure[18] for the Spanish, forcing the

Count-Duke of Olivares to resign at the beginning of 1643. In France, Richelieu was only just able to savour his victory; he died on 4th December 1642.

1.2 Geographical Considerations

Lleida (Lérida in Spanish and Lerida in English) is an old city, founded in the 6th century BC, and the capital of the Segría region. The city is located 155 km from Barcelona, 140 km from Zaragoza, and 465 km from Madrid. It is of Roman origin and was prosperous in the 13th and 14th centuries. By the 17th century the city had lost some of its prestige and was losing inhabitants. Following Passola-Tejedor [2004], the number of inhabitants was 6,000–6,500 in 1618, at the beginning of the Thirty Years War, and probably no more than 5,000 inhabitants in 1639, just before the start of the War of the Reapers. One of the reasons of this depopulation is probably explained by the strong resistance of the province of Lleida to the introduction of new agriculture techniques, especially irrigation channels. The city and its environs have a continental climate, with very hot summers in which temperatures can reach over 35° centigrade, and cold and dry winters with temperatures dropping below freezing.

In the 17th century the city lay on the north bank of the river Segre, between the hill of la Suda (i.e. turó de la Suda) and the hill of Gardeny to the west. It was protected by an old medieval wall enclosing the hill of la Suda (altitude 300 m) and a portion of the land between the two hills. A large stone bridge over the river Segre gave birth to the royal road to Barcelona. The surrounding territory was a dry, poor landscape with small orchards[19] (i.e. *Huerta* in Spanish) and little or no trees and where the main plant is the wild Thyme (*Thymus vulgari*), called locally *Timoneda d'alfes*. This plant is perfect for extensive agriculture, for the breading of sheep and goat. The Urgel valley nearby is a

---

[17] Pere Lacavalleria, *Relació compendiosa de tot lo que ha passat desde que lo exèrcit del rei de Castella ha partit de Tarragona y de la senyalada victòria que lo senyor mariscal de la Motte ha guianyada a la vista de la ciutat de Lleida.* [http://soltorres.udl.cat/jspui/bitstream/10459/1901/1/PLLE-1-0002.pdf].

[18] In Flanders, the Spanish army won the battle of Honnecourt on 26th May, but the destruction of the French army of Picardie had little effect on operations in Catalonia.

[19] Following Passola-Tejedor [2004], the *huerta* of the city of Lleida occupied an area of 9,000 jornals (1 hectare is equivalent to 2.29 jornales).

richer area, able to produce cereals, but the intermittent rainfall meant that production cannot be sustained year after year. Normally the main cities of the Catalan coast preferred to buy cereal in Sicily or Roussillon. To reach the city, the main roads were: the road connecting Lleida to Barcelona (Lleida, Tarrega, Cervera, Igualda, Martorell and Barcelona); the road connecting Lleida to Zaragoza (Lleida, Fraga, Bujador and Zaragoza); the road connecting Lleida to Tarragona (Lleida, Montblanc and Tarragona). From a military point of view, the environmental conditions meant that it was difficult to sustain and accommodate large armies in the province. Another drawback for Spanish forces was that the neighbouring region of Aragon was even drier, especially in the desert area between Zaragoza, Huesca and Fraga called the *desierto de los Monegros*.

In 1641, when a French engineer, Monsieur de Saint Pol arrived with the French garrison, he found a medium-sized city with virtually no modern fortifications. The French commander quickly recognised that Lleida would soon play an important role in the war with the Spanish Monarchy. To strengthen the defences, Cardinal Richelieu ordered the construction of a modern fortress on the hill of Suda. To carry out the construction, the French partially destroyed the old district of la Suda, maintaining only the old Cathedral. The districts of Cappont and Magdalena were also affected, but to a lesser extent. Due to a lack of money, time, and the resistance of the authorities of Lleida to the destruction of their city, the ambitious planned fortress had to be adapted to the topography and to the funding available. By 1644, a lot had already been done, the program of destruction had been finalised in 1642 and even if the city of Lleida was still protected by the old medieval wall, new fortifications were operational. On the hill, the core of the new fortress was finished in the spring of 1644 with the bastions of Cantelmo, Francès and Punxegut. The entrance of the main bridge of Lleida over the river Segre was covered by a half-moon on the south bank of the river. Around the rest of the walls key points, such as the

gates, were protected by provisional external fortifications, bastions, hornworks, and half-moons. When the Spanish besieged the city in 1644, only the half-moon of Cappont and the castle of Cardeny were attacked and taken with loss. The Spanish continued the construction of the main fortress and reinforced the gates by modern bastions made of bricks and rocks. The Spanish Governor Gregorio de Brito[20] created a new bastion behind the gate of the Infantes and isolated the fortress from the city. In 1647, Lleida was separated into three main defensive areas: the west city, the district of Magdalena to the east, and the fortress. The other important fortification was the castle of Gardeny on a hill west of the city. Originally it was a fortified tower of Templar origin with a small medieval wall. The French engineer had little time to modify it and in spring 1644, the castle had only been reinforced by external terrapleins and trenches to cover the main approaches. In 1645 and 1647, the Spanish built a ring of modern fortification mainly based on a hornwork and two small bastions. The new modern fortification was able to support a garrison of 400 men and was fully tested during the last siege. Even if the bastions covering the gates were mainly destroyed, the three main bastions of the fortress effectively supported the intense artillery fire and the fact that they were built directly onto the rock meant that theirs foundations could not be mined. In conclusion, the new defensive system of Lleida fulfilled its role to delay an invasion force and to give time to organise a relief army.

---

[20] Gregorio de Brito y Carvalhos, a nobleman of Portuguese origin (born 1600), died in 1648 in Zaragosa, from wounds received during the siege of Lleida.

Chapter 2
Structure of the Belligerent Armies

In the 1640s most of the major European armies were organized into three branches: infantry, cavalry and artillery. Infantry made up the bulk of the Spanish and French armies and was formed around a core of veteran units with a variable number of tercios or regiments made of raw recruits prone to desert as soon as possible. The cavalry had lost part of its prestige over the preceding centuries, but still attracted better quality soldiers than the infantry. Cavalry units tended to have proportionally more veterans than the infantry, but for the Spanish and French the problem was more related to the availability of good horses. The artillery was still a particular branch where most of artillerymen were not so much soldiers but rather civilians with specific skills.

After decades of continuous war, the Spanish government found it increasingly difficult to finance their military machine and had to contend with riots and rebellions. For the French monarchy the burden of the war was also tied to the lack of finance, and with the minority of the young king Louis XIV, the first minister Mazarin faced strong opposition.

In the field, the lack of money meant that some fronts had priority over the others, and that sometimes it was difficult to sustain enough men, weapons, and supplies to conduct offensive operations year after year. On the Catalan front the Spanish and French armies faced similar difficulties in trying to keep theirs armies together; this was in addition the problems caused by the particular nature of the geography around Lleida. One of the problems common to both armies was to find appropriate accommodation for the soldiers. As the war progressed, civilians in the frontier regions of Aragon, Valencia and Catalonia suffered continuously from the lack of discipline and cruel behaviour of the soldiers. All through the year, but especially during the winter, commanders received numerous complaints but normally could do nothing about them, mainly due to the lack of pay. Whatever the nationality of the troops, the peasants of these regions tended to view all soldiers as thieves and burdensome guests.

2.1 The Spanish Royal Army of Catalonia

Since the beginning of the 16th century, the Spanish monarchy had to put its faith in the creation of professional corps of infantry to control its immense territory. From a strategic point of view, the military forces of the Spanish Crown were located in a series of modern fortresses at key positions manned by mobile units of foot and horse. The tercios were the infantry formations; they were drawn from native Spaniards and numbered between 10 to 15 units for most of the 16th and early 17th centuries. They were situated in Italy (Lombardy, Naples and Sicilia) and Flanders – very few veteran troops being located in the Iberian Peninsula. In 1635, with the declaration of war on the French monarchy, the war erupted into the peninsular with operations in the Basque region, the viceroyalty of Catalonia, and on the Portuguese border. The need for troops increased drastically and the Spanish had to rethink the organization of their military forces. The traditional tercio units were not available in the peninsula and the monarchy had to rely mostly on new units raised by a levy on the militia of the different territories: Castilla, Aragon, Galicia, Valencia, Andalucía, the Basque country and Navarra.

2.1.1 The High Command

In the mid-17th century Spain was divided into the old kingdom of Castilla, the old kingdom of Aragon, the old kingdom of Navarra and the kingdom of Portugal. From an administrative point of view, when dealing with the defence of the realm, the old kingdom of Castilla was subdivided in nine General Captaincies, or *Capitanias General* in Spanish (*Canarias, Castilla la Nueva, Castilla la Vieja, Galicia, Extremadura, Jaen, Costa de Granada, Costa de Andalucia* and *Guipuzcoa*), and three other territories: *Principato de Asturia, Reino de Sevilla* and *Reino de Murcia*). The old kingdom of Aragon was divided in four vice-royalties: *Aragon, Catalonia, Baleares* and *Valencia*. Finally there was also the kingdom of Navarra. In each of these territories the king was represented by a *General Captain* or by a viceroy. The military structure of all these territories was similar with:

Spanish	English
Capitán General	Captain General
Gobernación de las Armas	Governor of the Arms
Maestro de Campo General	General *Maestro de Campo*
Capitán General de la Caballería	Captain General of the Cavalry
Capitán General de la Artillería	Captain General of the Artillery
Gobierno de Plaza Fuerte	Governor of Fortress

All these local commands were under the orders of a national administration: the State Council (*Consejo de Estado*), the Supreme Council of War (*Consejo Supremo de la Guerra*), the General Treasury of Spain (*Veeduria y Contaduria General de España*), the Captain General of Spain, the Captain General of the Cavalry of Spain and the Captain General of the Artillery of Spain. The Catalan front was supported by three vice-royalties (Catalonia, Aragon and Valencia). In 1643, at the commencement of our narrative, the vice-royalty of Catalonia was responsible for the cities of Tarragona and Tortosa and had command of the main battlefield army, called the Royal Army of Catalonia. The vice-royalty of Aragon was in charge of the

fortresses inside Aragonese territory and the vice-royalty of Valencia the fortresses located in the province.

2.1.2 Structures of the Infantry

Like all the Spanish armies of this time, the infantry fighting in Catalonia was a multinational army made up of native Spaniards (including the militia), national troops subject to the Spanish Crown (Walloons and Italians) and mercenaries (German and Irish).

Native Infantry
The Spanish infantry of the peninsula was governed by the Royal Ordinance of June 1632 which established that the tercios raised in the peninsula were to be composed of twelve companies of 250 men each. On 30th April 1633, the organisation of peninsular companies was a staff of 5 servicemen (a *Captain*, an *Alferez*, an Ensign (called an *abanderado*), a sergeant and a furrier), 6 non-service men (a fifer, two drummers, a furrier, a barber and a chaplain), 10 *cabos de escuadra*, 60 musketeers, 89 harquebusiers and 90 pikemen. This in theory gave 173 officers, including the senior officers of the tercios, and 2,856 *cabo de escuadras* and soldiers (744 musketeers, 1,116 harquebusiers and 1,128 pikemen). As we can see, these formidable numbers do not correspond to the normal tactical formation of 1640. A battalion of 500–1,000 men could be formed by one tercio, or by two or three amalgamated tercios. Also, some tercios were strong enough to field one or two battalions.[1] In 1633, with the war against the French monarchy rapidly approaching, the number of tercios available in the peninsula was next to nothing. The only forces available were companies serving either in the Armada (incorporated into the *Tercio de la Armada del Mar Oceano* and the *Tercio de la Armada de las Galeras de España*), or the companies in garrison in Portugal (in the *Tercio of Portugal*, also known as the *Tercio of Lisboa*). In 1634, in an attempt to establish a

---

[1] For example, at the battle of Leucate in 1637, the regiment (also known a *Coronelia*) de la Guardia fielded two battalions.

coherent mobile force, the Spanish created the coronelia of his Majesty (*Coronolia de su Majestad*) with 21 companies of 200 men and 16 regiments of noblemen of 1,375 men each.[2] According to Clonard [Vol 4] the recruitment of these noblemen's regiments was not executed properly and most of these units were not available for the service of his majesty. In 1635, the government created six new tercios,[3] but like the noblemen's regiments, the initiative was not successful. At the end of 1638, to support the operation around Fuenterrabia,[4] men were taken from the militia to form five provincial tercios[5] of 1,211 men each, distributed in 12 companies. This last system was more effective because it was financed by the militia, in other words, the villages, nobility and cities of Castilla could reduce the number of men conscripted by the contribution of a sum of money towards the tercio's pay. The last significant unit raised was the regiment of the Prince (*Regimiento del principe Balthazar Carlos*) in March 1642, which was formed from veterans living in Madrid and had 18 companies of 200 men each.

The infantry of the Armada,[6] integrated mainly in the two massive tercios mentioned above, actively participated in the defence of Catalonia. The Armada had some 1,500 to 3,000 infantry aboard the galleons and galleys of the Spanish navy. When the navy was not active, the Spanish would create temporarily marching tercios of 500 to 1,000 men to fight with the field army, or to garrison important fortresses such as Rosas, Lleida or Tarragona. They were known by the name of their Maestro de Campo, or sometimes by the name of *Tercio of Galeones* or *Tercio of Galleys*.

We have seen that by the treaty of *Union de Armas*, Catalonia, Navarra, Portugal, Aragon and Valencia were to contribute tercios to the royal armies. The money and the number of men involved were negotiated separately for each territory but both Catalonia and Portugal[7] were quick to refuse this burden and rejected the treaty. With the uprising in Catalonia in June 1640 and the rebellion of Portugal in December 1640, the Spanish government had to divide its peninsular forces between two fronts. The Catalan front had priority and Navarra, Aragon and Valencia sent their troops to this front.

Provincial tercios from Aragon, Navarra and Valencia

Under the *Union de las Armas* and others treaties, each of these territories had to supply a number of regular soldiers for the royal armies, troops that were for use in defending the kingdom and maintaining a militia. What is also important to understand is that a number of tercios had to be incorporated into the royal army each year. The vice royalties were responsible for paying the men of their own regular tercios for eight months

---

[2] The 16 regiments were raised by the high nobility of **Grandes de España**: *Conde Duque Olivares, Almirante de Castilla (Juan Alfonso Enriquez de Cabrera IX Almirante de Castilla), Condestable de Castilla, Duque of Medinaceli, Duque de Infantado, Duque de Nágera, Duque de Osuna, Condestable de Navarra, Conde de Niebla, Duque de Escalona, Duque de Medina de las Torres, Duque de Alburquerque, Duque de Sesa, Duque de Pastrana, Conde de Lemos and Conde de Oropesa* [Clonard, Vol 4].

[3] Following Clonard [op cit], the names of the Maestro de Campo were *Pedro Giron, Sebastiam Granero, Francisco de Megia, Cristobal Bocanegra*, the *Marques of Hinojosa* and *Francisco Manuel*.

[4] The siege of Fuenterrabia began in June 1638 when a French army of 21,000 men (Prince de Condé) supported by a fleet of 54 ships attacked the border city, which was defended by a garrison of 1,300 men. Spain organised a strong relief army, gathering all the troops available (some 16,000 men), and managed to breach the French lines. Condé had no choice but to withdraw his troops.

[5] The term "provincial" indicated that after a campaign most of the tercio was disbanded to be reformed the next year if the Cortes de Castilla could finance it. The Maestro de Campo were *Pedro de Giron, Domingo Eguia, Andres Pacheco, Diego de Caballero de Illesca* and *Francisco del Castillo*.

[6] Normally each active galley had a contingent of 60-70 infantry called a 'garrison'. In 1665, the formulae to calculate the minimal crew of a galleon were normally 1 seaman per 6.3 tons and 1 infantryman for 2.3 tons. In 1643, the 500 ton galleon *Santiago de Portugal* had 30 guns and a crew of 300 men (30% seamen and 70% infantrymen).

[7] For Portugal that is partially true because in 1639 a *Tercio of Portugueses* (Maestro de Campo Simón de Mascareñas) was created and sent to Roussillon for the siege of Salces. Another one (Maestro de Campo Pablo Parada) was created in 1640 and sent to garrison the city of Fraga in Aragon.

in the year, and the militia for two to four months. Finally, with the approval of parliament (*cortes* in Spanish), the king could raise troops in these territories to reinforce those tercios on the king's pay.

In 1640, the vice royalty of Aragon became involved directly in the war. The collapse of Catalonia had brought French armies to its eastern borders via the large plain along the valley of the river Segre. At that time Aragon had only 310,000 to 330,000 inhabitants. In 1641, the Spanish monarchy obtained agreement from the *cortes* of Zaragoza for the mobilisation of 4,800 men for six months at a rate above the ratio of one soldier per one hundred inhabitants that was applied in Castilla. In 1645 demands were more reasonable and the king only asked for the service of two tercios of 1,000 men each[8] in the royal army and payment for 500 additional men in the king's service.[9] Additionally, the king could call for the service of the militia for three months. Recruits to these tercios came mainly from outside the capital Zaragosa because that city had to raise and pay for its own unit for the army.

The vice royalty of Navarra had a frontier with France and had to maintain a number of troops to garrison the fortresses[10] of the province. Outside the province, Navarra contributed 4,000 men[11] to the defence of Fuenterrabia and between 1640 and 1642, Navarra raised, each year, two tercios of 1,000 men each for service in Catalonia. Later this was reduced to only one tercio of 1,000 men.

The vice royalty of Valencia had to defend its coast from North African pirates and had a complex system of 96 towers and defensive posts for that purpose. In theory Valencia could recruit 10,000 militia and in 1638 a tercio of 1,600 men was sent to Fuenterabbia. Later on, with the war in Catalonia, troops were sent to reinforce the garrisons of Tortosa and Tarragona. In 1645, Valencia and the king's council arrived at an agreement for the creation of eight tercios of infantry (*tercios del socorro de la frontera y defensa del reyno*, which could be translated as: *tercios for the assistance of the frontier and defence of the kingdom*) for service in the province of Valencia and at the frontier,[12] in total they numbered 5,000 men, 625 men per tercio.

National and Mercenaries Infantry

As we have seen, the possibility of raising 'veteran' troops from Spanish levies was unlikely and the royal Army of Catalonia had to rely on a mixture of national tercios and regiments of mercenaries. In 1637, the Spanish Council of War asked the governor of Flanders for two tercios of Walloons. The first tercio (Maestro de Campo Philippe de Gand, Comte of Isenghien) arrived in 1639 and it was followed in 1640 by that of Ghislain de Bryas, Marquis of Molinghen. These two tercios would participate in most actions in Catalonia over the period 1640-1652. During these campaigns they suffered heavy losses and were reinforced by new tercios throughout the decade; two of them were always available for service in the king's army. They were organised in the manner of Walloons tercios of the Army of Flanders.

Another important contingent was the troops raised in Naples. There were two tercios at the siege of Salses in 1639.[13] Later on, especially in 1642-1646, up to nine Neapolitan tercios were disembarked in Valencia or Vinaros. They suffered constant losses, mainly due to desertion, and had to be reinforced regularly over the decade. With

---

[8] From a review of April 1649 [Sanz 2007], the Tercio of Francisco de Sada had 10 companies with 56 officers and 606 soldiers (662 men), while the Tercio of Pedro Esteban Castellón had 10 companies with 52 officers and 697 soldiers (749 men).

[9] The new treaty established that Aragon would finance 500 horsemen for the next four years.

[10] Pamplona was the main capital and a modern fortress with a permanent garrison of 300 men.

[11] At the same time, to defend Navarra, the militia was summoned and some 9,000 men were raised to defend Pamplona and the mountainous borders. Exceptionally, as in 1638, Navarra temporarily raised 13,000 men.

[12] The frontier was obviously Catalonia and Valencia was supposed to support the king's army with 1,200 men [Pardo (1998), Militaria n°11, Universidad Computese de Madrid].

[13] The Tercio of Leonardo Moles and the Tercio of Jeronimo Tuttavilla.

the outbreak of fighting in Tuscany (1646-1647) and the uprising in Naples (1648-1650) the number of troops supplied dropped drastically. It is only after 1651 that troops from Naples could again be sent on a regular basis. Theoretically, Neapolitan tercios were organised into 15 companies of 200 men each.

On the Catalan front, the mercenaries were the Germans regiments[14] and the Irish tercios serving in this territory. Going back to Emperor Charles I (1519-1557),[15] Spain had a long tradition of using German mercenaries in their armies. For the Catalan front, German regiments were drawn mainly from southern Germany, sent to Naples via the Adriatic Sea, and later on to the province of Valencia. Another route would be to send the German regiments to Flanders and then by boat to Bilbao in the Basque Country. The long journey to reach the Catalan front meant that desertion and death would take a heavy toll on the German contingent before reaching Spain. Over the period 1643-1648, it is estimated that up to six regiments were incorporated into the royal army and three of them were probably available for active service or garrison duty.

Spain had used Irish mercenaries since the end of the 16th century and in 1638 two Irish Tercios[16] with 2,500 men disembarked in A Coruña. In 1641, and during the period 1643-1648, more men were transferred from Ireland to Spain. In the Spanish order of battle there were always two tercios[17] fighting with the field army or in garrison in Tarragona.

2.1.3. The cavalry

For the operations at Salses in 1639-1640 the Spanish High Command decided to reorganise the cavalry in the peninsula. Up to 1638 the main cavalry forces were the sixteen companies of Guardias de Castillas and the Cavalry of the Ordenes.[18] In April 1640, the Trozos of Roussillon was formed with the companies of cavalry based around Perpignan. It consisted of eight companies of 100 men and in 1643 was commanded by Andres de Haro. At the same time the Cavalry of the Ordenes was reformed and organised into a trozo. In 1642 a second trozo of Cavalry of the Ordenes was formed, but was integrated into the first trozo by November of the same year. The Military Orders were no longer a significant military force and the knights preferred to pay for replacements rather than to serve at their own expense. In 1641 a trozo of the Cavalry of Burgundy was formed in the province of Franche-Comté under the command of the Baron of Bouthier. During this period we can find a trozo called the Cavalry of Flanders, a trozo of cavalry from Castilla and a trozo from the Cavalry of Napoles. Finally there were some free companies to be found in the main garrisons; for example, in 1643, Tarragona had six

---

[14] In theory a German regiment consisted of a regimental staff (colonel, lieutenant-colonel, major, quartermaster, legal officer & provost with his men, surgeon with his assistants, chaplain and a wagon-master) and 10 combat companies. Each company had a staff or *prima planta* (captain, lieutenant, ensign, sergeant-major, quartermaster, sergeant, clerk, medical staff and two drummers or fifers), corporals, lance-corporals and 300 soldiers (120 pikemen, 30 calivermen and 150 musketeers). The regiment was supposed to have more than 3,000 men but, like the tercios in 1640, the German regiments never had more than 1,500 men when they landed in Spain. After some months of campaign, regiments were often reduced to just 400-700 men [J.L. Sanchez, web site].

[15] Charles I of Spain and Charles V of the Holy Roman Empire.

[16] The tercio of Tyrone had been in service since 1624; in 1638 the Maestro de Campo was Shane O'Neil, 4th Count of Tyrone, followed in 1641 by his son (8 years old) called Hugh Eoghan O'Neill, 5th Count of Tyrone. The other tercio was the Tercio of Tyrconnel with his Maestro de Campo Rory O'Donnell, 1st Earl of Tyrconnel.

[17] Tercio of Fizgerald (1640-1662), Tercio of Preston (1644-1646) and Tercio of O'Brien (1646-1670).

[18] In Spain the three main religious orders were Calatrava (founded in 1146), Santiago (founded in 1170) and Alcantara (founded in 1154). They were created to fight against the Muslim states and support the Christian kingdoms. In the 17th century the orders were more of a prestige association than a military force. The Conde-Duque Olivares tried to engage the Spanish nobility in the fighting in the peninsular, but by 1642, of the 1,400 Horse from the Cavalry of the Ordenes, only one-third were actually knights from one of the three orders. In subsequent years, some knights served as officers but most of the troopers did not belong to the orders.

companies of *Caballos Corazas* and *Arcabuceros a Caballos*.

In the peninsula by 1640, the Spanish cavalry consisted of *Caballos-Corazas* and *Arcabuceros a Caballos*. In line with trends followed by European armies, the Spanish cavalry progressively abandoned three-quarters armour in favour of lighter protection. Therefore, the *Caballos Corazas* lost armour and were equipped with only a front and back plates and a burgonet helmet, which was sometimes replaced by a wide brimmed hat.[19] Their main weapon was a pair of wheellock pistols, carried in holsters located each side on the saddle, and a straight sword designed for piercing and slashing. For the *Arcabuceros a Caballos* the principal weapon was a wheellock harquebus supplemented by a straight sword and a pair of wheellock pistols. They had little or no protection and relied instead on a buff coat or just a shirt to protect the thorax. For the head, the *Arcabuceros a Caballos* used a burgonet helmet, which was replaced most of the time by a felt hat. Their equipment was complemented by the necessary accessories for their harquebus: bullet pouch, priming flaks, powder flaks and wheel-lock spanner. Sometimes the differentiation between the *Caballos Corazas* and *Arcabuceros a Caballos* could only be made by the quality of the horses, the best ones being for the *Caballos Corazas*. The division between the two cavalry types was probably 20-30% *Arca-buceros a Caballos* and 70-80% *Caballos Corazas*. Dragoons appeared in Spanish service in 1632 as independent companies in the Army of Lombardia and later in the Army of Flanders. In the Army of Catalonia, we have mention of a tercio of dragoons in 1643, commanded by Antonio Pellicer. The unit disappeared in 1644 but it is possible that some companies of *Arcabuceros a Caballos* were performing their tasks.

2.1.4 Spanish artillery

Like all major European powers, the Spanish artillery of the beginning of the 17th Century consisted of multiple guns with different sizes or calibres. In 1609, the Spanish government decided to standardize artillery pieces into four calibres:[20] full-cannon of 40 pounds, half-cannon of 24 pounds, quarter-cannon of 10 to 12 pounds[21] and light guns, called quarter-couleuvrine or sacre, of 4 to 7 pounds. The first two calibres were heavy and designed to breach walls during a siege, the others could be used on the battlefield, but they were heavy. In 1620, the Spanish designed a new light gun called a Mansfelts or *Mansfelte* which normally fired iron balls of 5 to 6 pounds, or canister shot; together with the sacres, quarter-couleuvrine and quarter-cannon, they formed the field artillery.

On the Catalan front, Spanish artillery trains usually had 12 to 30 guns. For example, for the siege of Leucate in 1637, the Spanish army had an artillery train of 14 guns of 36 to 40 pounds, and 23 lighters ones from 2 to 12 pounds. In 1640, for the first attack on Barcelona, the army of Marques of Le Velez had an artillery train of 24 guns (probably half of them were light guns and the others being half-cannon and quarter-cannon) with 250 gunners. Later on during the war, artillery trains used to have 8 to 12 light guns for the field army and probably up to 30 guns for the army to use in siege operations. In August 1651, the siege train of 20 guns for the operation against Barcelona was composed of 2 half-cannon, 6 quarter-cannon, 6 sacres and 6 mansfelts.

2.1.5 The Spanish Army on the Battlefield

As we have seen the Spanish Army of Catalonia was made up of different nationalities organised into tercios or regiments, although the peninsular contingent

---

[19] With the hot weather in Catalonia during summertime, most of the horsemen tended to have wide hats with a steel cap under their hat rather than a closed helmet.

[20] In Spanish sources of the 17th and 18th centuries the calibre corresponds to the calibre of the cannonball.
[21] In reality you could find quarter-cannon from 10 to 16 pounds.

was predominant at 70 to 80% of the infantry. A variety of sources show that during the period 1643 to 1647, the main Spanish army could field between 8,000 to 10,000 infantry;[22] for example, in May 1644 9,500 men were drawn from 15 tercios and regiments, whilst in 1646, the Spanish needed 26 tercios / regiments to field 12,000 effectives. From 1641 to 1644, the average tercio was close to 670 men, while after 1645 the average dropped to 480 men. Excluding officers, the actual average number of men fit for service in a tercio was 580 men for the 1641–1645 period and less than 400 men after 1645. These tercios were formed with 6 to 20 companies, fielding 30 to 70 men per company.[23] Most of the time tercios and regiments were amalgamated into battalions; in May 1644, 6,000 foot were formed into 8 battalions (of 750 men each), 4 tercios formed 4 battalions, while 7 tercios and regiments were amalgamated to form the other 4 battalions. In September 1646, when the Spanish army marched out of Fraga, 12,000 foot were deployed in 15 marching battalions (of 800 men each) and each made up of one to three tercios and regiments. When the Spanish actually launched their attack on the French lines on 21st November, the 10 battalions had an average of only 500 men.

The ordinance of 1632 gave a ratio of 1 pike to 1.6 shot, however in the field the units tended to have less pikemen. The ratio was more usually 1 pike to 2.1 shot[24] (32% pikemen, 33% harquebusiers, 35% musketeers), or 1 pike to 2.3 shot. Normally, provincial tercios tended to have more harquebusiers and tercios of the nation more musketeers.

Tactically, for the 1643–1648 period, a 400-900 man battalion was formed by a block of pikemen, called the squadron, in the centre with their two 'garrisons' of harquebusiers;[25] this was supported by at least two *mangas* of shots (musketeers and harquebusiers). Depending on the number of veterans present and the number of men per battalion it is probable that the Spanish,[26] like the French, fought in 6 to 10 ranks deep. Also, depending on the circumstances, they tended to use *mangas* of shots to support the cavalry or to attack a key position. Finally, Spanish infantry could form special detachments[27] of 400 to 1,000 men for specific tasks. In Spanish they were called *escuadrón volante* (i.e. flying squadron) and to form this detachment pike and shot could be drawn from different tercios or regiments.

The Spanish Army of Catalonia, managed to field between 3,000 and 3,600 cavalry during the 1643–1648 period. In addition there were dismounted cavalry and companies in garrison. One of the major problems facing the cavalry was the lack of good horses. Aragon and Catalonia were not regions of grassland like northern Germany or the north of France. Forage was normally scarce and in wartime the situation was even worse; only a small number of horses could be maintained on campaign. Tactically, the Spanish cavalry was organised into squadrons of 100–150 horse made up of 2 or 4 companies.[28] In December 1640, during the

---

[22] In 1646, the Marques of Léganes probably had more than 12,000 infantry, but he quickly deployed some 4,000 men in Torre de Segre to secure his supply lines.

[23] In a review of the Army of Extremadura, in 1647 the company of Nicolas Tamayo from the regiment of Aguilar only had three officers and two soldiers.

[24] This calculation was derived mainly using data from the review of five Spanish tercios carried out in Perpignan in September 1639. [*Relación Verdadera de Todo lo Sucedido en los condado de Rosellon y Cerdaña*, Universidad de Sevilla, A 111/008(24)].

[25] A squadron could be formed by one or several tercios, depending on the tactical situation and the number of pikemen properly equipped (i.e. with armour – at least a front and back plate and a helmet) and present on the field. For example, during the battle of Santa Cecilia in November 1646, Pablo de Parada had in hand 1,000 men and formed a strong squadron of pike from four tercios to defend the entrance to Fort Rébé and placed the *mangas* of shots on the flanks.

[26] In Extremadura, during the battle of Montijo on 25th May 1644, the Spanish infantry numbered seven battalions of 610 men and fought in six ranks. It is most likely that the same tactical deployment was applied in Catalonia [Picouet 2010].

[27] During the battle of Montjuich in January 1641, the Spanish formed two flying squadrons of 1,000 musketeers/harquebusiers, one under the Duke of Tyrone and the second under Fernando de Ribera, to attack the fort of Montjuich [A.R. Esteban Ribas. *La batalla de Montjuich*. Magazine Desperta Ferro, Numero Especial 2011].

[28] From a review of the Army of Extremadura presented in July 1642, the average company had 4 officers and 39

operation of Cambrils,[29] Álvaro de Quiñ-ones's cavalry corps was composed of 4 squadrons of *Caballos Coraza* (11 companies) and 1 squadron of *Arcabucero a Caballos* (3 companies), in total some 600 horse.

2.2 The Franco-Catalan Army 1642-1648

Contrary to expectation, the size of the French force[30] in Catalonia was not small. Since the conquest of Perpignan in 1642, numerous contingents of troops were maintained in garrison (Perpignan and Collioure) in Roussillon and in the rest of Catalonia. These garrisons were maintained mainly in the towns and castles surrounding the city of Tarragona (e.g. Salou, Constanti, and Montblanc), in key fortresses in the centre of Catalonia (e.g. Flix, the castle of Cervera, Balaguer and Miravet) or along the Mediterranean coast (e.g. Palamos and Cada-ques). In other cities, such as Barcelona, garrisons were raised among the Catalans.

The French field army varied in size, depending on the needs of the government in Paris. When Mazarin wanted to restore French prestige after the defeats of 1644 and 1646, he sent significant sums of money, as well as troops, to form and maintain field armies of 13,000 to 15,000 men. Under the government of Richelieu, the French army had undergone a profound reform, adapting

aspects from the models developed by the Dutch and Swedes, as well as Germans and Spanish.

2.2.1 The Franco-Catalan High Command

From September 1641, the king of France was also the Count of Barcelona, and in Barcelona he was represented by a viceroy. This man shared power with the Catalan authorities,[31] but had sole responsibility for French troops in the province, as well as command of the field army that fought the Spanish. From 1643 to 1647, the vice-royalty was occupied by three men with strong military experience. Two of these men were of high nobility, demonstrating the interest of the French monarchy in the war in Catalonia. For the administration of the province, the viceroy was supported by a French administrator,[32] firstly René de Voyer d'Argenson from 1641 to 1643, and later by Pierre de Marca. From a military point of view, the viceroy had at his disposal a number of senior officers; norm-ally one or two *Lieutenans Généraux* (Lieu-tenant Generals), five to eight *Maréchal de camp* (Field Marshals), and the Governor of the arms of Catalonia – Josep de Margarit – responsible for the Catalan troops. Philippe de la Mothe-Houdancourt and the Count of Harcourt were the Marshals of France, but in 1647, the prince of Condé had the support of another Marshall of the France, the Duke of Gramont.

2.2.2 *The French Army*
The French infantry of the 1640–1652 period serving in Catalonia consisted of native French regiments and Swiss mercenaries.[33]

---

troopers (43 men in total), with the lowest (Company of Piñanrostro) at 2 officers and 7 troopers and the strongest (Company of Pedro Pardo) 5 officers and 61 troopers. Archivo General de Simancas, Guerra y Marina, Legajo 1460, "Relación detallada del número de infantería y caballería que forma parte del denominado *Real Ejército de Extremadura*, acuartelado en la ciudad de Badajoz y villas circunvecinas. Julio de 1642". In 1647 the garrison of Lleida had 505 cavalry, divided into 13 companies and giving an average of just 39 horsemen each.
[29] M. Parets, *Cronica de Cataluña*, Memorial Historico, Vol. 22.
[30] Following Michel le Tellier, State Secretary of War from 1643 to 1677, the French maintained 29,012 men in 1643 and 31,898 men in 1644. [*Michel Le Tellier et l'organisation de l'armée monarchique Par Louis André, Claude Le Peletier ou lettres de Mazarin*].

[31] The Catalan authority was the *Generalitat of Catalonia*, governed by Josep Soler (August 1641 – August 1644), Bernat de Cardona i de Raset (August 1641 – August 1644), Gispert d'Amat i Desbosc de Sant Vicenç (August 1644 – 5th March 1647) and Andreu Pont d'Osseja (August 1647 – August 1650).
[32] The title of d'Argenson was *surintendant de justice, police et administration*. The title of Pierre de Marca was *Visiteur Général de la Catalogne*.
[33] The following Swiss regiments are known to have served in Catalonia: the Regiment of Balthazard Am Büchel (10 companies), the Regiment of Nicolas Rhoom

From the French regiments, the so called Guards regiments,[34] *Vieux corps*, *Petit-vieux* and white flag regiments were permanent units with 30 companies and able to field one or two battalions. In 1636 [Thion 2009] we find six *Vieux Corps* regiments (Picardie, Champagnes, Piemont, Navarre, Normandie and La Marine),[35] six *Petit Vieux* regiments (known in 1643 as Nerestang,[36] Rambures, Auvergne, Sault, Vaubecourt and Beaumont) and eight regiments with a white flag (known in 1643 as Bellenave, Plessis-Preslins, Lyonnais, Montaussier, Nettancourt, Turenne, Hepburn and Chamblay). Other regiments had a nominal strength of 20 companies[37] and could field one battalion, or were amalgamated with another regiment to form a battalion of 600–800 men. These regiments were maintained by their colonel and could be disbanded at the end of the campaign.

On the Catalan front,[38] the white flag units were the regiments of Lyonnais, Champagne,[39] Nerestang (latter Saint Mesme) and

Vaubecourt (later Entragues). The other units were of diverse quality, depending on the name of their colonel. The regiments of the high nobility, such as Harcourt, de la Mothe-Houdancourt, Mérinville, or from the house of Condé (Enghien, Persan, Condé and Conti) were of the same quality as the permanent regiments, the others were from average to low quality. The arrival of the new recruits in April and May were important for enabling these last regiments to be of some use on the battlefield.

Cavalry

Most of the French cavalry was reorganized in 1638 [Thion, 2009] into regiments of nine companies (eight companies of horsemen and one company of Carabins, armed with a light harquebus called a *carabine*) of 70 men each. But, as stated by Thion, in reality few regiments had nine companies; most of them had only between four and eight companies with an average of 40 men per company. These regiments would form the core of the French cavalry in the Army of Catalonia. Close to them we also have the companies of heavy horses, companies of guards, companies of Chevaux-Légers and, of course, the companies of Gendarmes.[40] With up to 100 men per company, horsemen of these companies were also better equipped than the ordinary trooper. In the Army of Catalonia we would find two to four companies of heavy cavalry depending of the influence, charisma and fortune of the commander in chief.

Artillery

The French Artillery followed the same path as that of other European powers. From 17 calibres at the beginning of the 17th century, the number decreased to 6 in the second half of the century.[41] The French artillery was

---

(9 companies), the Regiment of Jacques Nicolas Praromann (12 companies), and the Swiss Guards (4 companies) at the sieges of Perpignan and Roses. In theory a Swiss company had 200 men – in reality, apart from the Guardes Suisses, the other four regiments had companies with less than 100 men.

[34] The Regiment of *Gardes Françaises* (30 companies of 200 men), the Regiment of *Gardes Suisses* (20 companies of 200 men) and the short-lived Regiment of *Gardes Ecossaises* (12 companies of 100 men), created in 1635 and disbanded in 1664.

[35] La Marine was the old regiment of *Cardinal-Duc* formed in 1635 by the Cardinal Richelieu. Richelieu changed the name to *La Marine* at the end of 1636. Between 1643 and 1647, François Le Hardy, Marques of La Trousse, was Mestre de Camp of the regiment.

[36] At the end of 1645, the Regiment was given to Anne Alexande de l'Hopital, Count of Saint Mesme, taking the name *Saint-Mesme*.

[37] From Corvisier, in the period 1643-1647, a French company had 3 officers (1 captain, 1 lieutenant and 1 ensign) and 70 soldiers; in 1643-1644, 40 soldiers; in 1645-1646 and 50 soldiers in 1647. The reality was companies of only 20 and 28 soldiers, excluding officers.

[38] On the Catalan front, due to losses and desertion, non-permanent French regiments might have only 10 to 15 companies [Belhomme, *Histoire de l'infanterie française tome 2*. French National Library].

[39] In June 1644, after the defeat of Lleida, in a letter, Pierre de Marca [*Memorial Historico* Vol. 25] urgently

asked for the arrival of the Regiment of Champagne to reinforce the weak French army.

[40] In 1659, all the existing companies of Gendarmes and Chevau-légers belonging to noblemen were disbanded and a new gendarmerie was created in 1667 by Louis XIV.

[41] In fact, by 1610, Sully had advocated having only six calibres, but in fact we have to wait for the reorgan-

divided into heavy artillery brigades with guns of 24 (le Serpentin), 30 (le Dragon Volant), 40 (le Dragons), 48 (Le Basilic) pounds, and light brigades with guns from 0.75 pounds (l'emerillon), to 12 pounds (l'Aspic). They had also guns of 16 (Passemut) and 20 pounds (la Couleuvrine). The artillery was one of the major arms on the Catalan front. For field operations, and especially for siege operations, the French were able to move a great quantity of heavy guns. The artillery trains were assembled in cities like Marseille and later disembarked in Barcelona and moved by wagon to participate in military operations.

2.2.3 Catalan Auxiliary Force

In October 1641 the Catalan authorities agreed to raise and maintain a native Catalan force, called the *batalló*, to support the French field armies in defending Catalan territory from attacks by the Royal Spanish Army. These forces could not be deployed outside Catalonia. In theory the *batalló* was made up of 5,000 Foot (five terços) and 500 Horse (five companies). In reality only half of the infantry would be available at any one moment and most of the time only for garrison duty. With the passing years, service in the *batalló* became unpopular and desertion rates were significant. Also, the collection of taxes to finance the *batalló* became more and more difficult, implying that the Catalan authority could not finance this force. In 1649, the Catalan field forces were converted into three French regiments[42] on French pay. Another Catalan force, the *somaten*, was also partially used during war. The *somaten* was a local militia that could provide up to 4,000 men[43] for a short period. They were organised into companies,

each based on a *vegueria*,[44] and could be called for the defence of an area of Catalan territory. Finally we have the urban militia from the main cities of Catalonia. The most important one was the Coronelia of Barcelona with up to 4,000 men and able to form four terços.

2.2.4 The Franco-Catalan Army on the Battlefield

In Catalonia, during winter period from December to March, French forces were mainly garrisoned in the castles and cities located on the front. Most of the cavalry and infantry had their quarters in the south of France. In April of each year, the cavalry would cross the Pyrenees to join the army near Barcelona or Cervera. Normally, the infantry would embark in France to be disembarked in Barcelona, before joining the army. In this way the French commander always had a field army available to him by the end of April. By contrast, in most cases the Spanish had more difficulty assembling their forces.

Following the trends of the war in Europe, the French infantry would normally form battalions of 700 to 900 men. Each battalion was made of one third pikemen, situated in the centre, and two thirds musketeers, situated on the wings. Commanded musketeers, called *enfant perdus* (i.e. lost children) could be deployed in front or elsewhere, for example with the cavalry. In combat the French tactic was to fire at close range, or point blank, followed by the attack of the pikemen. Following Thion [2009], the offensive was a recurrent characteristic behaviour of the French infantry. In Catalonia this was not the case and most of the time, in 1642, 1644 and 1646, the Spanish were on the offensive. On the Catalan front, the battalions tended to be smaller, 500 to 800 men, probably because most of the French infantry

---

isation of Louvois in 1679 for this to occur; these were: 32, 24, 16, 12, 8 and 4 pounds.

[42] Regiment of Josep de Margarit, Marques of Aguilar (1647–1660); Regiment of Josep d'Ardena i D'Arago (1647–1660); Regiment of N. Sénister (1647–1650).

[43] In 1646 a review by the French authorities gives between 2,400 and 3,400 men [Letter of Pierre de Marca to Le Tellier, 19th October 1646, BNF, Fond Baluze n°104, fol. 340].

---

[44] The *Vegueria* was a territorial demarcation of medieval origin, corresponding to a county, shire or bailiff in English. In the 17th century the Principality of Catalonia was divided in 20 *Vegueria*s.

regiments had less than 20 companies due to the high desertion rate.

On the battlefield the French cavalry was organised into squadrons, three to six deep. Many French cavalry officers had served with the Swedes or the Germans of Bernard of Saxe Weimar and favoured the charge with sabre, using their pistols for mêlée, especially when battle was underway. On the Catalan front it appears that the French cavalry tended to be more numerous and probably better disciplined than the Spanish.

One of the powerful branches of the French army was the artillery. On the battlefield the French tended to have more guns and heavier ones than the Spanish. This is due to the fact that it was easier to bring guns from Barcelona than from Zaragosa or Madrid. It is noticeable that de la Mothe-Houdancourt in 1644, Harcourt and Condé were able to bring with them more guns, either for siege or for the battlefield, than their Spanish opponents.

2.3 Weapons of the Belligerents

As in all early-modern armies, the infantry was armed either as pikemen or as musketeers. For the pikemen, the individual weapons of the Spanish and French soldiers were the pikes, swords, and sometimes daggers. In the Spanish army, the pike was 5.0 to 5.4 m long while in French service the pike was somewhat smaller at 4.2 to 4.6 m (13 to 14 French feet). The Spanish also used other arms, such as the halberd, partisan and *chuzos*[45] when fighting occurred during a siege or to take/defend a fortification. Pikemen were supposed to wear full-armour, consisting of gorget, breast and back-plates, pauldrons at the shoulder, tassets at the belly and groin, and a helmet. In fact, only veteran soldiers from the tercios or from German regiments were correctly armed, other pikemen probably only had a helmet, breast and back-plates. In French service, only Swiss regiments retained full-armour; French regiments tended to have little armour, probably only breast, back-plates and a helmet.

For musketeers, Spanish soldiers could be armed with a harquebus or musket, swords and daggers, while French soldiers had muskets and swords. Catalans tended to be armed like the Spanish. When one reads original sources concerning the armament of tercios in the 17th century, the word harquebus appears regularly. Why were the Spanish still using the harquebus when this weapon had disappeared from most European armies at the end of the 16th century? According to a number of sources, both ancient and modern [Albi de la Cuesta, Quatrefages, Cristobal Lechuga], in the first half of the 17th century, the Spanish harquebus typically fired a spherical lead bullet[46] of ¾ to 1 oz.[47] The gun barrel was between 95–100 cm, giving a total length of around 120-130 cm, and a weight about 4-5 kg, so no fork was needed. The range of the weapon is given as 200–220 m, but after 75 m it was imprecise. A typical Spanish musket weighted between 7.5 and 9 kg and perhaps more (> 10 kg) in some cases. The typical bullet weight was 1½ or 2 oz. and the gun barrel was around 120 cm (±5 cm), for a total length of 140–150 cm. In short, the Spanish harquebus of the war in Catalonia was a light weapon, perfect for short range fighting (< 70 m). Against armoured troops or at longer range (100 m), the Spanish had their ordinary musket firing one of the heaviest lead balls in Europe.

By the decade of the 1640s, the French army was using only muskets; an ordinary musket, probably similar to the one introduced in 1600 by the Dutch, firing a bullet of 40-42 g (10 to 12 to the pound) weighting 7.0 to 7.5 kg and using a fork. The other musket was lighter, following Louis de Gaya (1678),

---

[45] The *chuzo* was a simple short pike of 2–2.5 metres, typically used aboard ships and galleys of the armada.

[46] Normally each soldier received a "pasta" of lead and a mould called *turquesa* to make their bullets. Because each soldier was making his bullets, they were small variations between bullets and the shape of the bullet was not a perfect sphere.

[47] The oz in Castilla was 28.75g, in Milan 27.38 g, in Valencia 22.19 g, in Viscaya 30.50 g, and in Zaragoza 21.88 g.

it had a length of 151.7 cm, a barrel of 119.2 mm, a weight of 6.2 kg (no fork), and fired a bullet of some 40 g. Other muskets made in Germany were probably used, Engerisser (2009) gives the description of a light German musket with a length of 142 cm, a barrel of 102.5 cm a weight of 4.2–4.7 kg and which fired, in theory, bullets of 35 g.

For all belligerents, the weight of the lead bullet is probably overestimated. Archaeological evidence from the battle of Rakovnik in November 1620,[48] in which tercios from the Spanish army participated (the Walloon tercio of Bucquoy and Neapolitan tercio of Spinelli), indicate that the real weight was smaller than expected. At Rakovnik the average weight for a musket bullet was 25 g and for an arquebus 19 g. From the Edgehill battlefield [Foard 2009] musket bullets had a weight from 27 to 40 g and caliver/arquebus bullets a weight from 21 to 26 g.

So a Spanish arquebus was probably firing bullets of 16 to 23 g, and a Spanish musket bullets of 24 to 47 g. A French musket was probably firing a bullet of 30 g (16 to the pound), with a maximum weight of 35 g.

---

[48] Personal communication from Pavel Hrnčiřík.

Chapter 3
Campaigns from 1643 – 1647

3.1 The Situation in Aragon in September 1643

As we have seen, the Catalan front has been the grave of the Count-Duke Olivares and the hope of quickly reducing the revolt of the Catalans vanished in 1642. Catalonia was now another playground for the two catholic powers. So what was the situation of these two enemies in Catalonia in September 1643?

At that date, the Spanish army[1] had probably 23,000 men in Catalonia, 12,000 of which could go on campaign. The rest was divided into some 4,000 men in garrisons in Southern Catalonia[2] (Tortosa and Tarragona), 3,000 men in the fortress of Rosas, the strong garrison of Fraga and others small garrisons[3]

in Aragon – probably some 4,000 men. The main officers of the Army of Catalonia were Don Felipe de Silva[4] as General Captain, Don Juan de Garay as Maestro de Campo General, Don Francisco de Orozco and Marques of Mortara as Generals of the Cavalry and Don Geronimo de Tuttavilla as General of the Artillery. Others officers were Don Fernando de Tejada, Lieutenant-General of the Cavalry of the Army of Aragon and Don Alvaro de Quiñones, Lieutenant-General of the Trozo of the Ordenes.

On the Franco-Catalan side, the victories of 1641 and 1642 had reinforced the authority of the viceroy, Philippe de la Mothe-Houdancourt. Unfortunately for the French commander, with the death of the Cardinal Richelieu in December 1642, he lost his main support at the French court. Furthermore, the death of King Louis XIII on 14th May 1643, had given ground to the regency of the queen, Anne of Austria, supported by Cardinal Mazarin. The new strong man at the head of the French state had little affinity with de la Mothe-Houdancourt, thus reinforcing the distrust between them. In June and July 1643, the French army conducted minor operations in the County of Ribagorza, taking, for example,

---

[1] From a letter from 11th August 1643 [*A. Valladares de Sotomayor, Semanario Erudito que comprehende ... Volume 33 pages 11 – 111*] the Spanish expected to bring together 23,000 men in Aragon: 12,500 from the royal army (Spanish, Walloons and Italians), 4,000 from Aragon, 2,000 from Valencia, 2,000 from Andalusia and 2,500 veterans of the Army of Flanders, the squadrons which capitulated at Rocroi in May 1643.

[2] The *aviso* of 1st September 1643 (A. Valladares de Sotomayor, *Semanario Erudito.... Vol 33*) gives a garrison of 3,500 Foot and 250 Horse in Tarragona and we can estimate a garrison of 500 men in Tortosa.

[3] In 1643 Aragon had to protect three main areas against the French. The first was the Pyrenean border covered by the Castle of Canfranc, the modern fortress of Jaca, with a garrison of 400 men and the small fortress of Santa Elena near Biesca. The second was the County of Ribagorza and the eastern border of Aragon, protected by the Castle of Benasque, the Fortress of Ainsa (with a garrison of 60 to 100 men), the castle of Monzón (in French hand in 1643), the city of Fraga (garrisoned by up to 3,000 men) and the castle of Mequinenza (garrisoned by up to 500 men). The third area corresponded to the south bank of the river Ebro,

protected by the fortress of Caspe and the Castle of Alcañiz. Of course there were other medieval fortifications (city walls or castles) of little use in the wars of the 17th century.

[4] Felipe da Silva y Silva was born in 1589 in Portalegre (Portugal) and died in February 1646 in Zaragoza. He had a long career in Spanish service – he was Captain General of the Cavalry of Lombardia and Maestro de Campo General of the Army of Lombardia in 1637. In March 1643, he took the command of the Army of Aragon from the Marques of Leganés.

the medieval castle of Benabarre on 8th July, but the main threat against the city of Barbastro on the river Cinca never materialised. At the end of July a Spanish cavalry force conducted a raid against French quarters south of Lleida, inflicting losses on the French army.[5] With little movement from the French,[6] the Spanish commander decided to take the initiative. The first movement was a tentative one to take the city of Flix, on the river Ebro, by surprise. Intelligence had shown that the city had a small garrison of less than 300 men, and Juan de Garay proposed sending a select force of 3,500 Foot and 500 Horse, supported by a small flotilla of 12 river boats with 500 musketeers. The infantry was provided by two Spanish tercios (the Regiment of Guardia del rey and the Tercio of Martin Mujica), the Italian tercio of Tito Brancaccio, and a new German regiment. The cavalry was provided by the Trozo of the Ordenes (*Fernando de Tejada*) and the cavalry of the general commissar Blas Janino. The small corps set out from Fraga on 8th September but had to withdraw on receiving the news that a force of 500 Frenchmen had just entered the city of Flix. At the end of September 1643, the Spanish field army was between Zaragoza and Fraga. On 21st October, Felipe da Silva decided to move north and join his force of 8,500 Foot, 3,000 Horse,[7] 300 dragoons with an artillery train of 20 guns near Barbastro. At first he moved the army to Tamarit and Alguaire, north of Lleida. De la Mothe-Houdancourt moved French forces[8] to observe the Spanish and on 25th October a small skirmish started between the two cavalry forces. Felipe de Silva did not want to engage in battle and withdrew cautiously to Fraga. In this city, the Council of War decided to attack the city of Monzón and by 29th October the entire army was before this objective. In just a few days the Spanish constructed lines of circumvallation and took up positions to the south of the hill where the castle was located, installing a battery of six guns. Two weeks after the start of the siege Felipe da Silva received some reinforcements from Aragon. Meantime, de la Mothe-Houdancourt also received reinforcements from the Catalan government, and by the middle of November had gathered at Alguaire some 2,500 Horse and 8,000 Foot, including 2,000 Catalans, but did not move. In Monzón the siege continued and on 1st December, Felipe da Silva informed the French governor that four mines were in position with 460 barrels of black powder, ready to explode. The next day the governor capitulated on the condition of being allowed to remove himself and his men to Lleida. The French commander decided to evacuate the rest of the French force from their positions in the County of Ribagorza and to fortify Lleida. With the arrival of the cold and the snow on the mountains, both armies went to their respective winter quarters.[9]

3.2 The 1644 Campaign: the First Siege of Lleida

The Spanish Council of State had to give priority to the war in Catalonia and the king of Spain, Felipe IV, agreed to move with a reduced court to support operations in this region. The other fronts would take a defen-

---

[5] The Aviso of 3rd August 1643 [*Memorial Historico* Vol. 33] claims that French losses were 1,500 dead and wounded, and 1,000 prisoners. These numbers are exaggerated.

[6] In reality, with the death of Richelieu in November 1642, de la Mothe-Houdancourt lost popularity at the French court and he was always complaining of the lack of funds to continue the campaign. It seems that one of the objectives of the French was to take the city of Tarragona. A French fleet of 24 vessels and 12 fire ships, under the command of Marquis de Brézé, arrived in Barcelona in August, but the attack on Tarragona did not occur. Instead the French naval squadron went to the south and successfully intercepted a Spanish squadron of 25 ships (13 galleons, 3 urcas, 8 frigates and a smaller ship) at the battle of Cartagena on 3rd September (Spanish losses were 3 galleons and one urca).

[7] Some authors [Anale de Cataluña and Il mercurio] increase the number to 10,000 Foot and 4,000 Horse.

[8] An estimation of the French army gives only 2,000 Horse and 6,000 Foot.

[9] Following the Gazette de France of 1644, de la Mothe-Houdancourt had in January 1644, 16 infantry regiments: 6 in Lleida, 3 in Balaguer, 2 in Flix, 1 in Miravel, 2 in the Empurdà and 2 in Villafranca.

sive position, especially in Flanders,[10] to resist French armies. Felipe IV left Madrid on 6th February and arrived in Zaragoza on the 13th. With the arrival of the king, the build-up of the army speeded up and on 1st May 1644, Felipe da Silva presented his field army to the king at Berbejal, 7 km south west of Barbastro. The Spanish had assembled an infantry force of 1,209 officers and 8,345 soldiers with Spanish,[11] Walloon,[12] Italian,[13] and German[14] contingents. The rest of the army was made up of a strong cavalry force[15] of 378 officers, 3,356 mounted troopers and 602 dismounted men. Finally the artillery train had 6 heavy guns and 10 quarter-cannon (10 pounders) and up to 8 mansfeltes (5 pounders). The commanders of the army were Felipe da Silva as General Captain of the Army of Catalonia, the Marques of Mortara as Maestro de Campo General,[16] Don Juan de Vivaro as General of the Cavalry and Francisco Tuttavila as General of the Artillery. The contingents from Aragon and Navarra were enroute, or in garrison along the Catalan border.

On 2nd May, the king[17] presided over a parade of his army marching to the south of Barbastro. The next day a strong bridge was built across the river Cinca, and by midday on the 4th, all the army had crossed the river. On the 6th the army was in Tamarit de Litera, and the next day, the entire army crossed the river Noguera in Alfarràs. On 8th May the vanguard of the army was observed by some enemy scouts and took the town of Castelló of Farfanya without resistance. The city of Balaguer now lay just 8 km to the east. The same night, Silva arrived with the army and formed a strong vanguard, under the command of Juan de Vivaro with 3,000 horse and 500 musketeers. The task of Juan de Vivaro was to find an unguarded ford to the south of the city and to cross the river Segre. On 9th May, the task was done and Felipe da Silva could send 3,200 infantry from eight tercios and regiments (Tercio of Mujica, Tercio of Brancaccio, the two Walloons tercios and the four German regiments) to reinforce Vivaro's troops.

On 11th May, Juan de Vivaro's corps of 6,500 men and two light guns (Mansfeltes of 5 pounder calibre) was deployed near Termens and marched north to block the bridge of Balaguer. On the French side,[18] Philippe de la Mothe-Houdancourt had news of the Spanish preparation thanks to an effective network of spies. Lleida had a good garrison of six regiments (probably 2,500

---

[10] In 1644, a powerful French army under the command of the Duke of Orléans commenced operations against the coastal cities of Flanders, particularly Gravelines. The Spanish Army of Flanders was still a powerful force, but even with support of the mercenary army of the Duke of Lorraine, they could not check the advance of the French from the south and the Dutch from the north.

[11] Six Spanish tercio, each forming one battalion: the Regiment of the Guardia del Rey, commanded by Simón de Mascareña; the Regiment of the Principe, commanded by Nuño Pardo de la Casta; the Tercio of Mujica, commanded by Don Martin de Mujica o Muxica; the Tercio of Ascárraga, commanded by Don Esteban de Ascárraga; the Tercio of Villamayor, commanded by Don Alsonso de Villamayor, and the Tercio of Freire, commanded by Don Francisco Freire.

[12] Two Wallon tercios, each forming one battalion: the Tercio of Calonne, commanded by Charles Antoine de Calonne and the Tercio of Van der Straeten, often called Brandestrat, commanded by the André Van der Sraeten.

[13] Three Neapolitan tercios, each forming one battalion: the Tercio of Amato, commanded by the Baron of Amato; the Tercio of Brancaccio, commanded by Frey Tito Brancaccio, and the Tercio of Laurenzana o Lorenzana, commanded by the Duke of Laurenzana.

[14] Four German regiments, forming two amalgamated battalions: the Regiment of Galaso; the Regiment of Glosflet or Grosfeit; the Regiment of Ludwig Haumel, and the Regiment of the Baron of Seebach.

[15] The Cavalry probably had some 100 companies (40 squadrons) coming from six trozos / regiments: the Trozo of Rousillon (commanded by Andres de Haro); the Trozo of the Ordenes (commanded by Juan de Oto); the Cavalry of Flandes (commanded by Blas Janini); the Cavalry of Napoles (commanded by Ferdinand Limonti); the Regiment of Burgundy (commanded by the Baron of Bouthier) and a contingent of the Old Guards of Castilla (commanded by Don Roque Matamoros).

[16] The Lieutenants of Maestro de Campo were Pedro de Valenzuela, Gaspar de Mesa and Alonso Garnica.

[17] For three days the King had the command baton of the army and on 4th May he returned it to Felipe de Silva. It was the first time that a king effectively commanded a Spanish army on campaign since the time of Felipe II.

[18] The chronology of events prior to the battle differs somewhat in the Gazette of France from 1644. This French source indicates that by 13th May the Spanish already had some fortifications on the east bank of the river Segre.

men) of infantry, supported by 600 militia; the new citadel was partially operational. Balaguer had a smaller garrison with three regiments of infantry; the main problem for the French commander was that his field army was weak because every year he had to wait for new recruits from France and the forces raised by the Catalans. At last, on 5th May, a naval squadron of 20 warships (9 galleons, 9 galleys and 2 smaller ships) escorting 40 merchantmen arrived in Barcelona with 5,000 Foot and war supplies. On receiving news of the Spanish movements, de la Mothe-Houdancourt sent a message to his troops to join Cervera 45 km west of Balaguer as soon as possible. French patrols detected the movement of the Spanish army and 800 men were drawn out from Lleida on 9th May and urgently sent to reinforce the city of Balaguer. More forces were sent from Cervera to reinforce the garrison. These last forces arrived between 10th and 11th May, and when Vivaro's troops came in view of Balaguer, by the night of 11th May, the city probably had a garrison of up to 3,000 men. The news of the arrival of all these reinforcements took Felipe da Silva by surprise and he urgently sent an order to Vivaro to halt his advance and retire to Térmens.

Next day, the Spanish commander gave another order to Juan de Vivaro, to take up positions in front of Lleida and to occupy Vilanoveta.[19] These arrived on 13th May, and occupied a fortified position around the town. Meanwhile Felipe de Silva was with the main army, including the artillery, and found himself delayed by heavy rains.[20] He spent 13th May blocked by the swollen river Noguera some kilometres south-east of Albesa. The situation was urgent because the French army was closing in and was now west of Bellpuig, just 30-35 km from Lleida, and preparing to reinforce the garrison with supplies and troops. Felipe de Silva, decided to send another force under Simon of

Mascareña with 1,000 Foot (the Regiment of the Guardia del rey and four *mangas* of musketeers) and the rest of the Cavalry to occupy the ford of Corbins on the river Segre. This was done during the night of 13th/14th May. When the French vanguard of 2,000 men appeared in the morning, they found the Spanish in a good defensive position and retired. The Spanish commander received intelligence that de la Mothe-Houdancourt probably had some 7,000–8,000 infantry and 1,800 cavalry[21] and was coming with the intention of fighting[22] to introduce reinforcements into the city of Lleida. Time was running out, Felipe da Silva and the council of war decided to unify Spanish forces on the east bank of the river Segre. The construction of a boat bridge, 1.8 km north-east of Lleida, was undertaken to join the infantry with Vivaro´s forces. At dawn, the first tercio crossed the river and was soon joined by the others. On the morning of 15th May the Spanish force was deployed as follow:

- North of Lleida, we find the rearguard under the command of Francisco Tuttavila, with 300 Horse, the Tercio of Villamayor, the Tercio of Ascárraga, two German regiments (Haumel and Seebach), the main artillery, the baggage and supplies.

On the other side of the Segre, Spanish commanders organised the main force of 6,000 Foot and 3 000 Horse as follow:

- The right flank was commanded by Juan de Vivaro, with the Cavalry of Flandres, the Trozo of Roussillon, the Cavalry of

---

[19] It is possible that some of the infantry, especially the German regiments of Haumel and Seebach, went back to the main army.

[20] Vivaro's force also suffered from the rain but they only had two light guns and so could advance faster.

[21] Following Miguel de Parets [*Memorial Historico* Vol. 24] de la Mothe-Houdancourt only had 7,000 Foot and 1,500 Horse. Gonzalo et al. [1997] gives 9,000 Foot and 2,000 Horse.

[22] In French documents [*Letters of Pierre de Marca* and *Letters of Mazarin*] it is said that another batch of reinforcements (3,000 men, including the Regiment of La Marine) had landed at Barcelona by 19th/20th May. The urge to challenge the Spanish army in battle probably had several causes: firstly de la Mothe-Houdancourt had been criticized for his inaction during the 1643 campaign; secondly, even with this reinforcement, the total was 13,000 men and with this force it would have been difficult to force the Spanish lines of circumvallation; finally, the fortification of Lleida was not completely finished and the garrison of 2,000 men was not strong enough to resist a siege.

Burgundy and an infantry battalion formed by the Regiment of the Guardia Real.

- The centre, commanded by the Marques of Mortara, had a line of two Spanish infantry battalions (the Tercios of Nuño Pardo and Mujica), one amalgamated Walloon battalion (the Tercios of Calonne and Van der Straeten), one amalgamated German battalion (the Regiments of Galaso and Glosflet) and one amalgamated Italian battalion (the Tercios of Brancaccio and half of the Tercio of Amato).

- The left, commanded by the Marqués of Cerralbo, had the Trozo of the Ordenes, the Cavalry of Napoles, the Cavalry from the Old Guards of Castilla and an Italian infantry battalion (the Tercio of Laurenzana and the other half of the Tercio of Amato).

- The reserve was formed by a battalion of the Tercio of Freire and four Mansfeltes (5 pounder light guns), forming a battery on the left.

- Finally there was a detachment under the command of Pablo Gil de Espinosa with 300 musketeers from all nations and a company of cavalry guarding the access to the main bridge of Lleida.

On the French side, de la Mothe-Houdancourt deployed his army on a hill 3 km east of Lleida. The French deployment is less well understood, but there were probably eleven infantry battalions, formed into two lines, and covered by two wings of cavalry. The artillery of 10 or 12 guns was installed in front of the infantry in two batteries. The infantry was formed from the seven French regiments, namely the regiments of Lyonnais, de la Mothe-Houdancourt, d'Albret, Mompouillan, Vandy, Rébé and Chastellier-Barlot, probably two Swiss regiments (the Regiment of An-Buchel and probably that of Jean Jacques Rhan) and two tactical Catalan battalions (one commanded by the Baron of Carpotella). The cavalry had 14–16 squadrons from the guard company of de la Mothe-Houdancourt, and six regiments (la Mothe-Cavalerie, Baron d'Alais, Bussy-de Vair, de Villeneuve, du Terrail, de Roches-Baritaut and Balthasar). The right wing was commanded by the Lord

of du Terrail and the left by the Lord of Boissac.

Around midday, the Spanish army started its march following a parallel route to the French position at a distance of 1 km from the French batteries. Noticing the Spanish march, the French artillery opened fire, sometimes with success, killing whole ranks of soldiers. The Spanish movement surprised the French officers, some of them were even thinking that the Spanish did not want to fight and were retreating to Tarragona. In fact, de la Mothe-Houdancourt was probably thinking that Felipe da Silva was trying to outflank his exposed right and he ordered the second line to move to the left. With the extension of their front, the French force could now form a continuous line. After 90 minutes of moving under artillery fire, taking casualties, the Spanish army finally stopped and faced the French position. The Spanish commanders reorganised their battalions into one line and the cavalry squadrons into two lines. Next, all Spanish forces crossed a small ditch full of water and advanced directly towards the French position.

The first encounter took place when the Spanish cavalry of the right flank met incoming French squadrons. At first the combat was inconclusive, but when Juan de Vivaro launched the three squadrons of the second line, the Spanish succeeded in driving back the French. On the left, the battalion formed by the regiment of la Guardia de Rey, was following the cavalry of Vivaro and chose to attack the battery of the French left flank defended by the regiment of de la Mothe-Houdancourt. On the Spanish left wing, the Spanish cavalry managed to advance up the hill. The French squadrons positioned resisted unsuccessfully and started to give ground rapidly. The remainder of the Spanish infantry battalions attacked the centre of the French line covered by the infantry. On the Spanish right, the regiment of de la Mothe-Houdancourt battled fiercely, fighting with their pikes to contain the Spanish. But the push of pikes produced by the elite of the Spanish tercios was too much for the French and the men from the regiment of de la Mothe-Houdancourt started to give ground. In the French centre the infantry regiments made a poor showing against the incoming Spanish forces. Their musket fire was ineffective and most of the time they refused to fight with their pikes. With no reserve behind, and the partial destruction of the regiment of de la Mothe-Houdancourt, the French first line began to crumble and panic quickly spread among the French soldiers. On the left wing, the Spanish infantry and cavalry occupied the top of the hill while the rest of the regiment of de la Mothe-Houdancourt was completely defeated. In less than one hour, the French commander had lost control of his troops and could only think of how to escape.

While the main fighting was taking place between the two armies, the French governor of Lleida prepared a force of 600 men to attack the small detachment of Pablo Gil de Espinosa. The French infantry crossed the bridge by surprise, killing all the Spanish soldiers they encountered, and therefore securing access to Lleida. In this short action more than 100 Spanish lay dead.

On the south of the hill of the battlefield, the Marquis of la Valière had still some coherent forces to hand and de la Mothe-Houdancourt saw the opportunity to push reinforcements inside Lleida. He sent the Marquis of la Valière and a strong detachment of French troops, including the debris of the regiment of Lyonnais, to make contact with the garrison of the city. Although pursued by the Spanish cavalry the French managed to safely enter Lleida. On the battlefield, the French infantry still had three battalions withdrawing slowly in direction of Borgues Blanques. The Marques of Mortara sent Juan de Vivaro with some squadrons to attack them. Seeing that the Spanish cavalry was close to them, the French infantry lowered their weapons and surrendered. The last French force left the battlefield leaving behind hundreds of prisoners, their luggage, and all the artillery. The dream of the French commander of repeating the battle of 1642 had ended in disaster.

Following French sources, de la Mothe-Houdancourt's decision to confront the Spanish army with an incomplete army was the key of his defeat. It is true that thousands of French soldiers were still in France and could only arrive at the beginning of June, but the French general had in hand 10,000 men with 12 guns and held a favourable position. On the Spanish side, the performance of the cavalry and the infantry had been excellent. Even if 2,000 men,[23] under Vallière, managed to reinforce the garrison of Lleida, the outcome of the battle was terrible for the French. They had lost some 3,500–4,000 men,[24] all their artillery, and the baggage. On the Spanish side losses were some 400–500 men, mainly due to the effect of artillery fire. To this number we could add the loss of some 100 men from the small detachment guarding the bridge.

The first benefit from the victory was to boost the morale of the Spanish and Felipe da Silva sent a letter to the inhabitants of Lleida calling on them to surrender. However, one of the consequences of the battle was the entrance of French infantry into the city, and the French governor now had close to 4,000 men,[25] enough men to resist. A formal siege had to be undertaken and the Spanish began to deploy their army for the task. Felipe da Silva organised it into two main quarters and three smaller ones. The first was located to the north-east of Lleida, in a place called Secá de San Pere, and was called the quarter of the King (Cuartel del Rey); this had most of the troops and supplies. A battery of four heavy guns was placed in front of this position, which covered the approach from Balaguer. To the south of this fortification, the boat bridge on the river Segre was covered by a redoubt with infantry from Aragon. On the other side of the river was the second large quarter; located in Vilanoveta, it was occupied by the Trozo of the Ordenes, the Guardia of Castillas, the Spanish tercio of

---

[23] Sources diverge on numbers, but 2,000 men seems to be a good compromise. Of these numbers, not all men were fit for battle, and an appreciable proportion had either lost their weapons or were wounded, and thus unfit for action. The next day, in Lleida, the regiment of Lyonnais had only 25 officers and 439 soldiers, half of their original number.

[24] French source, such as the *Gazette de France 1644*, give losses of 2,000 men.

[25] Following a letter from Pierre de Marca [*Memorial Historico* Vol. 33], dated 25th June 1644, the French garrison had 181 officers and 3,575 men inside the city.

Mujica, the two tercios of Walloons and the four German regiments. The distance from Vilanoveta to the river and the boat bridge was covered by the quarter of the Molino, occupied by the Tercio of Ascárraga. To cover the approach from the north, the Spanish established the quarter of Villamayor. Trenches and palisades were constructed between the different quarters.

The first important action took place on 22nd May with the assault on the half-moon of the Cappont that protected the entrance to the stone bridge. The first attack expelled the French and the Spanish organised the defence with three *mangas* (Spanish, Walloons and Germans) of 150 men. With artillery support from three light guns, the garrison counter-attacked and managed to retake the position. The Spanish launched a second attack and this time they held the position. The half-moon was fortified to resist artillery fire from the city and the Walloons from the Tercio of Calonne occupied the position. Three batteries with guns and mortars were established, one in Cappont, and the other two to the north of the city.

On the French side, the humiliation of the battle on 15th May could not be tolerated by the new head of government, Cardinal Mazarin, and he managed to find both money and reinforcements and sent them as quickly as possible. When these reached Barcelona, de la Mothe-Houdancourt reorganised his field army of 9,000 men. At the beginning of June he established his camp between the Noguera and the Segre rivers, to the south-west of Balaguer. Several times, the French commander sent small detachments to try to slip supplies in the city, but most of the time these tentative efforts failed, and the blockade was maintained by the Spanish. On the south bank, between Vilanoveta and the quarter of Molino, the line of fortifications was reinforced with a new quarter called the Casina Blanca; this was occupied by the Tercio of Mujica. In the hot summer of Lleida, the siege was difficult for the Spanish to maintain; the casualty toll, due to combat,

illness and desertion was significant.[26] However reinforcements were on their way: Castilla was supposed to send 6,000 infantry and horses for the dismounted cavalry. The 3,000 men from the militia of Aragon were now operational and would be sent to Lleida. Also in June, 1,200 men from the Tercio of Valencia, commanded by Jéronimo Mansiuri, and 1,000 men from the Tercio of Navarra, commanded by Baltasar de Rada, were expected. Of course, of the 11,000 men allocated to reinforce the Army of Catalonia, probably less than two-thirds actually arrived.[27] On 10th June, Francisco Tuttavilla launched a massive attack on the fortress situated on the top of the hill of Gardeny with the Tercios of Villamayor and Brancaccio. At first the attack was successful, but the French counter-attacked with 2,000 men and retook the position, inflicting serious losses (200 to 300 men) on the Spanish. Felipe da Silva decided to modify his plan of attack; four days later the Spanish (Regiment of the Principe) managed to take a windmill and a convent between the hill of Gardeny and the city. At the same time the Spanish were digging approach trenches and galleries to place mines against the French position. Seeing the danger, the French garrison launched another counter-attack to dislodge the Spanish, but this time the position around the windmill was maintained in Spanish hands and the attackers had to withdraw back to the city. Although the mine encountered rocks and could not continue, Tuttavilla introduced barrels of black powder in full view of the French commander of the fortress of Gardeny, and on 16th June sent him an invitation to surrender. The stratagem worked and the Spanish infantry took possession of the fort the following day.

After the defeat of May, de la Mothe-Houdancourt had to do something to restore his prestige among the Catalans and in front

---

[26] At the end of May, Spanish commanders estimated their forces at 5,000–5,500 Foot and 2,000 Horse on active service around Lleida.

[27] When the Tercio of Valencia arrived in Fraga on 15th June, it only had 600 men, excluding the officers [relación de la Campaña de 1644 en Catalunya, CODOIN 95].

of Mazarin. Now he had enough men, and he decided to cut the Spanish supply lines where they crossed the river Segre, in front of the town of Torre de Segre. Part of the plan required the city of Lleida to send small boats to enable the crossing of the river. From their spy network in Barcelona, the Spanish discovered the objective of the French and Felipe da Silva organised the defence of the town, reinforcing the position of le Cappont with more guns and musketeers and sending a force of 2,000 Foot and 800 Horse under the command of Don Carlos de Padilla to defend Torre de Segre. On the night of 18th May, the French garrison made different attacks to confuse the Spanish, but they failed to send the boats and de la Mothe-Houdancourt had to withdraw to Balaguer. After this episode, the Spanish constructed a second wooden bridge over the Segre to facilitate communications with the quarter of Vilanoveta, and installed a battery of eight medium guns in the fortress of Gardeny. Inside the city the situation became critical and the French governor had to reduce the food ration. On 7th July a mutiny of the inhabitants of Lleida was suppressed, but the situation inside the city remained tense. Ten days later, de la Mothe-Houdancourt again occupied the position between the Noguera and the Segre rivers. This time the objective was to send fireboats down the river to destroy the main Spanish bridge to the north east and then to attack the Spanish positions. Launched on 19th July, the attack failed, due to heavy musket and artillery fire, which destroyed most of the fireboats. The small fire that was started on the bridge was quickly put out by the Spanish. The following day de la Mothe-Houdancourt crossed the river Noguera and deployed his army only 1.5 km from the Spanish lines of circumvallation. Behind this line, the Spanish general followed the movements of the French with most of the Spanish army. The French general had few options, and seeing that the Spanish were waiting for him, he slowly withdrew to his previous position. De la Mothe-Houdancourt remained for seven days at a distance of a dozen kilometres from Lleida, but on 26th July, he moved his army to the south of Barcelona. The French governor of Lleida

understood that the city could not resist any longer. Negotiation started the same day and on 30th July the city capitulated to Felipe da Silva. Next day, the French forces marched out with their flags and two small guns, and on 7th August, the King of Spain, Felipe IV, made a triumphal entrance into the city. The new Spanish garrison consisted of some 4,000 men, coming from the provincial tercios of Aragon and Valencia.

At the beginning of August, the situation was paradoxical. The victorious Spanish army was exhausted after a long and difficult siege, while the defeated French army, located near Barcelona, was ready for action with all the reinforcements[28] having now arrived from France. To complicate the situation, Felipe da Silva resigned his command and Don Andrea Cantelmo was nominated Viceroy of Catalonia and General Captain of the army. On 7th August, de la Mothe-Houdancourt reorganised his army[29] into two corps; he deployed a small force to control the approaches to Barcelona and with the rest he moved to besiege the city of Tarragona on the Mediterranean Sea. After losing Lleida, the French commander thought that a success against Tarragona could restore his reputation and the morale of the Franco-Catalan forces. At that time, Tarragona had a garrison of 3,000 men[30] commanded by Don Francisco Torralto. De la Mothe-Houdancourt immediately initiated operations, with the

---

[28] These consisted of the regiment of Champagne with 30 companies; five regiments (Nérestang, Vaillac, Vervins, Tavannes and Toulongeon) from the army of Guyenne, as well as 1,000 Horse; three new regiments raised in May (Ferron, Cauvisson and Ruvigny), and new recruits for the regiments in Catalonia. From June to July, the French sent 10,000 men and 16 artillery pieces to rebuild the French Army of Catalonia.

[29] An estimation of the French army in front of Tarragona gives 12,000 men, supported by a Catalan auxiliary force of 400 horse and 1,000 Foot (Tercio of Josep Sacosta and Tercio of Alexo Semmanat).

[30] Infantry: the Tercio of Lisboa (Spanish), commanded by Diego de Aguilera, the Tercio of Pablo Parada (Spanish), the Tercio of Clemente Soriano (Spanish), the Tercio of the Earl of Tyrone (Irish), the Tercio of Pierre de Mande (Walloon), some German companies under the command of Captain Millane, two companies of the city militia and one company from Tortosa. The cavalry consisted of 300 Horse in eight companies.

support of a powerful French fleet[31] under the command of Admiral Brézé. On 13th August a battery of eight guns began firing at the Spanish fortifications to the south of the city near the sea. The objective was to occupy first the harbour to prevent the arrival of supplies and reinforcements, and then to attack the city. On 22nd August the Spanish sallied out of the city and managed to inflict losses on the French, destroying six guns. On 25th August the French launched a double attack: from the sea disembarking 900 infantry, and from land, to take the jetty. The operation was a partial success and the French managed to blockade the harbour. On the Spanish side, on 10th September, Andrea Cantelmo moved his army of 12,000 men (9,000–10,000 infantry and 2,600 cavalry) to support the defenders of Tarragona. The following day a key council of war took place in the French camp. The French commanders knew that the Spanish army was on the move and that no circumvallation lines had been constructed to resist an attack. It was decided to abandon the siege of Tarragona and to move the army to cover the castle of Cervera and the road to Barcelona. On 13th September, the governor of Tarragona observed the departure of the French army, the siege had cost 3,000 French and more than 500 men for the Spanish.

With his manoeuvre, Andrea Cantelmo had achieved his goal, the siege was lifted and the Spanish commander withdrew to the west, taking Balaguer in few days, followed by Agramunt. Most of the Urgell valley returned to the obedience of the King of Spain, even if significant resistance continued at the fortress of Àger in the Pyrenees, defended by a tercio of 500 Catalans from the *batalló*. At the beginning of November, Cantelmo sent the Spanish army into winter quarters and de la Mothe-Houdancourt was recalled to France where he was arrested.

3.3 The 1645 Campaign: the Battle of San Llorens of Montgai

After the successful campaign of 1644, the King Philip IV returned to Madrid and the command of the Army of Catalonia was given to an Italian officer, Andrea Cantelmo. In 1645, the first task of Cantelmo was to provide Lleida and Balaguer with appropriate garrisons, to reinforce their fortifications, and to reduce the burden on Aragon for the accommodation of troops. During the spring, a rough estimate of all the forces in garrison in Rosas, Tarragona, Tortosa, in the region of Lleida, and in Aragon would be close to 13,000 men. On the French side, Mazarin could not tolerate these defeats; the political situation in the province was not good and some Catalan peasants were viewing the behaviour of French soldiers to be as bad, or even worse, than the Spanish. Also, the Spanish had supporters in a section of the elite of Barcelona who wanted to overthrow the Franco-Catalan administration. Mazarin sent money and troops to rebuild the French Army of Catalonia. In January 1645, the count of Plessis-Praslin received orders to move to Perpignan with part of his army. The French decided to attack the fortress of Rosas, defended by a garrison[32] of 2,000–3,000 men under the command of Don Diego Cavallero. The French army (7,000 infantry[33] and 1,000 cavalry) arrived on 2nd April in front of Rosas. They were supported by naval squadrons amounting to 20 ships (12 ships, 4 fire ships and 4 boats, commanded by the

---

[31] The French fleet had 20 galleys, 22 warships, 10 fire ships and 11 smaller ships [C. de la Roncière. *Histoire de la Marine Française* tome 2, Paris 1920]. The fleet heavily supported the operation against Tarragona, firing 5,814 iron balls, especially on 25th August.

---

[32] In 1643, the garrison had 3,000 Foot (the Tercio of the Armada and the Tercio of Diego Cavallero) and 300 Horse. In 1645, the Venetian Ambassador [Nani] in Paris indicated that the garrison had only 2,000 Foot and 300 Horse on active duty. In his memoirs the Marques of Chouppes [*Mémoire du Marquis de Chouppes*] gives 3,000 Foot and 500 Horse.

[33] The French infantry was probably formed by 14 French regiments (Lyonnais, Normandie, Navailles, Saint Paul, Duke of Ventadour, Marquis de Tavannes, Huxelles, Sault, Chaussoy, Vaubécourt, Mérinville-Infanterie, Calvière, Marquis de Vandy and Chastellier Barot), 2 Swiss regiments (4 companies from the Gardes Suisse and regiment of Praromann) and 1 Catalan battalion.

Lord of Montigny), supported by 10 galleys (the squadron of the Baron of Baumes) to block the arrival of supplies and reinforcements from the sea. Despite the efforts of the garrison, on 10th April the French managed to install a battery of 10 guns and started to fire at the main wall between the bastion of Saint John (San Juan) and the bastion of Saint George. Unfortunately for the Count of Plessis-Praslin, two days later a strong thunderstorm and heavy rains started and continued for four days. Most of the French trenches were drowned and the French fleet lost two galleys. Plessis-Praslin and Harcourt reorganised the French forces, and with the arrival of more troops, the operation against Rosas was begun again on 19th April with 10,000 men. Over the course of five weeks, the French slowly approached the main walls. This was achieved under intense fire from the fortress, coupled with frequent attacks from the garrison. The Spanish command organised a number of operations to get supplies to the garrison. For the Spanish garrison, salvation could only come from the sea, but the Spanish armada was unable to organise a sufficiently powerful naval squadron in time to challenge the French fleet. Finally, on 25th May, a mine was detonated, destroying part of the walls; four days later Diego Cavallero capitulated with the honours of the war. The 1,500 men from the garrison were transported to Cartagena.

With Rosas in French hands, Harcourt could reorganise the French Army of Catalonia and initiate operations in the direction of the river Segre. The first objective was the town of Agramunt, which was taken with little resistance.[34] At that time, Harcourt's army[35] was made of 8,500–9,000 French infantry (probably eighteen infantry regiments), 2,400 cavalry (Company of Gendarme, Company of Guards and eight regiments) and 1,200–1,500 Catalans (two battalions).

After the surrender of Rosas, Andrea Cantelmo moved with his army to protect the Spanish position on the upper Segre. At that time the main Spanish field army probably had 11,000–11,500 men,[36] divided into 8,000 infantry and 3,000 cavalry. The infantry was distributed between 11-13 units coming from three Spanish tercios (Provincial of Navarra, Pedro Valenzuela and Pedro Osteriz), two Walloon tercios (Count of Gransfelt and Van der Straten), the Irish Tercio of James Preston, five Italian tercios (Fray Brancaccio, Baron of Amato, Duke of Laurenzana,[37] Poctiques and Baron of Mata),[38] and probably two German regiments (Baron of Seebach and Felipe Seugmedia o Soumandra). The cavalry was made of the Trozo of the Ordenes, companies from the Cavalry of Napoles (commanded by Miguel Pinateli and Tiberio Garaffa), and probably companies from the Cavalry of Castilla, and from the Trozo of Roussillon.

At the beginning of June, five infantry units (Osteriz, Gransfelt, Preston, Seebach and Seugmedia) of the Spanish army fortified themselves behind the river Segre, in a mountainous region between Camarassa and San Llorens. A small detachment of 200 men, from the Tercio of Gransfelt, was guarding the Castle of Camarassa on the other side of the river. The rest of the army (7,000–7,500 men) was between Lleida and Balaguer. At first Harcourt sent a vanguard under the command of Monsieur de Saintonge with three infantry regiments (Nerestang, la Marine and Le Ferron-Infanterie), a Catalan battalion and two regiments of cavalry (Harcourt-Cavalerie and Baron of Alais). On 15th June this vanguard attacked the Castle of Camarassa. The defence did not last long and the Walloon captain surrendered the castle to the French. For the French army the next step was to cross the river Segre, but they found that the west bank of the bridge of Camarassa was well defended by Spanish forces. With the help of local peasants, the French

---

[34] From contemporary accounts there is no evidence that the Spanish garrison was important, Agramunt was probably only an outpost with less than 100 men.
[35] In his memoirs Plessis-Besançon gives for the infantry 800 officers, 7,500 soldiers, 2,400 horse and 1,500 Catalans [*Mémoire de Plessis-Besançon*].

[36] *Memoirs of Novoa* in CODOIN volume 86.
[37] In Spanish sources this is often written as the Duke of Lorenzana. Italian sources give the name of Alfonso Gaetani, Duke of Laurenzana.
[38] These last two tercios are cited by Parets in *Memorial Historico* Vol. 24.

commander found a small undefended rope bridge some kilometres to the north. Quickly the French sent more troops to the other side of the river and marched south through mountainous terrain. During the march, the French infantry encountered pickets of Spanish forces from the Regiment of Seebach and the Tercio of Preston. After a short fight, the French column managed to defeat, one by one, the overstretched Spanish infantry. On 18th June the Spanish forces around the bridge of Camarassa were attacked from the front and the rear, and after a crude defence, most of the Spanish were dead or prisoners,[39] the rest fleeing to San Lorenz. The defence of Camarassa and the position on the river Segre had cost some 2,000 men (dead, wounded, prisoners and fugitives) for the Spanish; the French army had lost only 300 to 400 men. Harcourt now had in hand the bridge of Camarassa and, after some repairs, he crossed the river on 21st June with most of his army, leaving a detachment consisting of the Catalan battalion, the regiment of Nerestang and some companies of cavalry on the west bank of the river.

Harcourt initiated the movement of his army at 3 a.m. on 22nd June and marched behind the mountain to arrive in front of the plain of San Llorens at 9 a.m., where the main part of the Spanish army was deployed. When Andrea Cantelmo received the news of the defeat of his force, he deployed his 7,000–7,500 men (3,000 Horse and 4,000–4,500 Foot) in a plain 1.4 km to the south-west of the village of San Llorens. The Spanish were deployed in two main groups: a vanguard near a mountainous pass with probably two Italian tercios (Poctique and the Baron of Mata) and cavalry from the Trozo of Ordenes; the bataille with the core of the cavalry comprised of two Spanish tercios, three Italian tercios, supported by three companies from the Tercio of Osteriz, as well

as Irish companies from Tercio of Preston. Some detachments were also positioned to defend the village of San Llorens. With all the Spanish artillery withdrawing to Balaguer, the aim of the Spanish general was probably to gain enough time to get his army safely under the walls of Balaguer. At first the French cavalry encountered the Spanish vanguard on the mountain and, after a short fight, the Italians and the Trozo of the Ordenes were swept from their positions, fleeing in panic into the plain.

Pushing his force as quickly as possible through the pass, Harcourt deployed his troops into two corps, mixing infantry battalions and cavalry squadrons. On the left, commanded by the Count of Chabot, there were four cavalry regiments (Mérinville-Cavalerie, Roches Baritaut, Boissac and Le Ferron) and eight infantry regiments (La Marine, Vaillac, Montpouillan, Roquelaure, Mirepoix, Montpeyroux, Anduze and Saintonge); On the right, commanded by Mérinville, there were three cavalry regiments (Harcourt-Cavalerie, Saint-Simon and de la Mothe-Houdancourt) and probably six or seven infantry regiments (Harcourt-Infanterie, Champagne, Rébé, Pailler, Mérinville-Infanterie, Ferrière and probably Beaufort). Harcourt was in the middle with the cavalry regiment of Alais, his Life-Guard company, and his company of Gendarmes. Finally, the Swiss regiment of Rhoom was behind in reserve. In total the French had 2,000–2,200 Horse and 7,000 Foot.

The French commander ordered a full-scale assault by his two corps onto the main Spanish force located in the plain. The Spanish had no choice but to receive the full weight of this attack. At first they managed to repulse the French, but after two hours of heavy fighting, most of the cavalry was retreating to the south, while the infantry was pushed toward the river. Some of soldiers tried to cross the river but they were either shot down by the Franco-Catalan infantry positioned on the other side, or they were drowned. At last, in order to avoid a complete massacre, the Marques of Mortara surrendered, along with probably 2,000–2,500 of his men. Spanish losses were horrendous, and following different French and Spanish

---

[39] Following Lacavalleria [*Relació de Verdadera de tot lo que ha succehit al Exercit de sa megestat en Cathalunya y lo que ha passat al passer il riu segre* .... 22 June 1645. In V. Balaguer. *Historia de Cataluña tomo 14*], during this last day the Spanish lost 800 dead and wounded and some 1,000 prisoners. During this fighting, the Spanish lost a lot of men, especially from the Tercios of Osteriz and Gransfelt, and the Regiment of Seugmedia.

sources, the Spanish army had lost in six days of intense fighting between 6,000 and 7,000 men, including some 2,000 dead and drowned, 3,500–4,000 prisoners, and hundreds made into fugitives. The survivors of the defeat withdrew to Balaguer where Cantelmo was able to gather[40] some 4,000 infantry and 2,500 Horse. For the French army losses were lower, probably between 600 and 800 men. After the battle, the Count of Harcourt regrouped his troops around San Lorens; for a number of days he was short of supplies and he had to move the numerous Spanish prisoners to Barcelona. With the arrival of supplies and reinforcements, Harcourt had now an army in a condition to besiege Balaguer. By 5th July most of the city and its garrison was encircled by the victorious French army. Harcourt did not want to take the city by force, the defending forces were too numerous, so the French started to slowly occupy positions to blockade the city.

Andrea Cantelmo was trapped in Balaguer with most of his army; he was relieved of his command of Captain General, but was still in charge of the defence of Balaguer, while Felipe da Silva was recalled to be given command of the whole Spanish army. In the second week of August, a series of clashes occurred when the Spanish tried to introduce supplies into the city. At the end of August, and after talks with the high command in Lleida, Cantelmo decided to escape from Balaguer with most of the cavalry. During the night of 25th August, some 2,000 men (1,300 cavalry and 600 musketeers) divided in two groups and went out of Balaguer. The rearguard encountered French detachments, resulting in some fighting, but the Spanish managed to join with the garrison of Lleida, losing only 100 men in the process. The rest of the garrison of Balaguer was put under the command of Simon Mascareña with orders to resist as long as possible. The Spanish, now under the general command of Felipe da Silva, commenced various diversions to support the garrison of Balaguer. At the same time, the Spanish received intelligence that the city of Flix, on the river Ebro, was ill defended, with only a garrison of 150 Frenchmen. An expedition was quickly organised with some 400–600 cavalry and 1,500 infantry, mainly from the regiment of Ludwig Hamel. On 27th October, at dawn, the city was attacked and taken after a five hour fight. The French commander reacted quickly and organised his forces into three corps; one to maintain the blockade of Balaguer, one to deal with the small army of Felipe da Silva, and the last one, under the Command of the Count of Chabot, to retake Flix. On 2nd September the count of Chabot was in front of Flix with 2,000 men. The Spanish forces were defeated, losing hundreds of men in the process, and the city was retaken by the French commander. The failure of Flix was the last setback of the Spanish army that year. The list of defeats was increasing, disillusion was growing, and the morale of the Spanish army was sinking. In Balaguer, Don Simon of Mascareña was still holding out, but the fate of the city was sealed. After a siege of 14 weeks, Mascareña finally capitulated on 20th October, principally due to a shortage of supplies. For the French commander the victories of 1645 had restored the prestige of the French army and the Count of Harcourt could return to Barcelona to restore order to civilian affairs[41] and prepare for the 1646 campaign. On the Spanish side, Lleida and Tarragona were still in their hands, but for how long? Money was scarce and the pressure on the diverse Spanish territories, especially in Flanders, was terrible.

---

[40] These numbers probably take into account the garrison of Balaguer and the survivors of the field army.

[41] During the summer and autumn of 1645, Barcelona was a city full of spies and plots against the French and Catalan authorities. The Count of Harcourt had to act with severity against the traitors of the Franco–Catalan cause.

3.4 The 1646 Campaign: The Second Siege of Lleida and the Battle of Santa Cecilia

At the beginning of 1646, the Spanish *valido* Luis de Haro[42] recognised that the heavy defeats suffered throughout the previous year meant that the only viable strategy was to adopt a defensive position around Lleida and Fraga to the east, and Tarragona and Tortosa to the south. In January 1646, the new governor, Don Gregorio de Brito, entered Lleida and quickly took a series of measures to prepare the city, and the population, for a long siege. While men were sent to Lleida to enhance the fortifications, supplies were gathered in Zaragoza. In February and March, large convoys were sent from Zaragoza to Fraga and Lleida. This proceeded slowly, partly due to bad winter weather and partly due to continuous French raiding parties. But little by little, Brito was able to accumulate supplies, weapons[43] and troops in the city. By the middle of March he had enough men to adopt an aggressive defence against the French cavalry. This tactic provoked a number of clashes between the two sides. The largest one occurred at the beginning of April when Brito and the cavalry of Baron of Seebach organised a raid against Térmens, one of the positions where Harcourt was storing supplies for his offensive. On 6th April, late in the afternoon, 2,000 Foot and 200 Horse from Seebach's force and the garrison of Lleida, advanced quickly on Térmens, defended by 1,200 men. Brito at first sent 20 men to create false alarms. Four times, the small Spanish force advanced and retired as quickly as possible, the fifth time, all the men of Brito's command

were with them. In a matter of minutes the Spanish soldiers, covered with white shirts,[44] scaled the walls and overpowered the few French guards. By dawn 800 Frenchmen and Catalans of the garrison surrendered, the others lay dead or had escaped to Balaguer, the *encamisada* was a total success. Brito managed to return to Lleida, unhurt, and with his prisoners.

In spite of the failure of the Trémens garrison, Harcourt finally launched his campaign on 28th April. The core of the French army marched out of Barcelona in direction of Cervera. Here Harcourt divided his army[45] into two corps, one to Ballaguer and the other to Bellpuig, to confuse the Spanish commander. On 2nd May the Marques of Leganés sent a letter to the Governor of Tortosa warning him to be prepared should the French army appear before his walls.

The main concern of the Spanish commander was the news that a convoy with 20 small boats was in Balaguer. Brito was asked to send 1,000 men (two tercios) from the garrison to reinforce the positions on the river Cinca, in case the French intended to attack Aragon. On 9th May, the French northern corps crossed the Noguera and arrived in front of Alguayre; at the same time, 2,000 men from the northern corps occupied Corbins and the troops stationed in Bellpuig moved south in the direction of Vilanoveta. The small castle of Alcarraz was taken on 10th May, and on 11th May, it was the turn of the Castle of Albatarech on the south bank of the river Segre. The same day, Brito asked for the return of the 1,000 men, but the next day, the Spanish commander could see that French troops were surrounding Lleida – the siege had started. On 12th May, Gregorio de Brito officially had

---

[42] Luis Menéndez de Haro y Sotomayor was a Spanish politician; born in Valladolid in 1598, he made a career at the Spanish court under the protection of his uncle, the Count-Duke Olivares. In 1643, he replaced him as valido, or favourite, as the king's confidant. He never had the same power of his uncle but he managed to end the war with the negotiations that led to the treaty of the Pyrenees in 1659. He died in Madrid in 1661.

[43] Brito managed to accumulate food, troops, small-arms, musket balls, black powders, but he was less lucky concerning the number of guns and cannonballs.

[44] The Spanish called these operations *encamisadas* from the name for shirt in Spanish, *camisa*.

[45] Sources on the French army are confusing. Gonzalo et al (1991) gives 9,000 Foot and 3,000 Horse, but indicates that these were the troops in Balaguer; the troops of Bellpuig are missing. Pradet [*Memorial Historico* Vol. 24] gives 12,000 Foot and 5,500 Horse for the French army without the Catalans. Possibly the northern corps in Balaguer had 12,000 men, and the force around Bellpuig 5,000 men.

4,400 men:[46] 500–600 men were in the fortress of Gardeny, modernised at the beginning of the year, 3,000 were on active duty in Lleida, and some 700–800 men were unfit for service. Lleida also had 25 guns, but only 3 of them were of a heavy calibre (one 40 pounder and two 24 pounders), 12 guns had a calibre between 7 and 10 pounds and the final 9 had a calibre below 5 pounds. From that date, the French started the construction of a line of circumvallation of 26 km in length, with three main quarters. To the north-west was the quarter of Couvonges, to the north-east, the quarter of Harcourt, also called the quarter of the king, and to the south, the quarter of Chabot (later called Mérinville) around Vilanoveta. In between, the French constructed a series of trenches, small fortresses and smaller quarters. While all this work was taking place, Harcourt ordered an attack on the half-moon of the Cappont, defending the bridge of Lleida. On 17th May the count of Chabot attacked the Spanish position, but they met with fierce resistance, and with the arrival of reinforcements from the city, and the death of Chabot, the whole operation ended in failure. For Gregorio Brito, this success was important; it meant that the French could not efficiently bombard the city from the south bank. At the beginning of June, Harcourt decided that the city would be starved out. On 30th May a convoy with more small boats arrived and Harcourt sent them to form a new bridge over the southern length of the river, to connect the quarters of Couvonges and Mérinville.

In Fraga, the Marques of Léganez was despatched to form an army to confront Harcourt, but in May he was obliged to reinforce all the garrisons along the river Cinca and could barely muster 6,000 men for his field army. To distract the French general, he sent a message to Francisco Tuttavilla in Tarragona requesting that he execute a diversion. Tuttavilla took 2,000 Foot, 400 Horse, and two light guns with him and marched to Montblanc, the main city of the Conca de Barberà. Harcourt was quickly notified and sent 500 Horse, as well as some infantry companies, to support the defence of Montblanc. The Spanish column encountered significant opposition from the Catalan *somaten*[47] of the locality, losing up to 300 men, and preventing Tuttavilla from reaching his goal. Frustrated by their failure, the Spanish soldiers took their revenge on the peasantry, committing atrocities in some villages of the Conca de Barberà. In Lleida the siege continued and Harcourt received reinforcements[48] from France and Barcelona. At the beginning of June an operation was carried out to take the town of Alguayre; the lines of circumvallation were also finished. The French spent part of the month of June reinforcing their fortified lines with new trenches, palisades, small earth and wood forts, as well as wood huts for the troops. Unfortunately for the French soldiers, the summer of this year, 1646, was hot and dry. For the numerous soldiers and civilians living in painful conditions around the city, this weather was a disaster. The difficulties of finding drinkable water lead to dreadful illnesses, such as dysentery. These appalling conditions, coupled with the continuous fighting against the garrison, lead to an increase in the rate of desertion, thus significantly weakening French forces. On the other side, governor Brito did not remain immobile. The garrison made constant sallies to disrupt the construction of the lines of circumvallation and to try to destroy the bridges. The biggest one took place on 23rd June when 1,400 men attacked the bridge of Grenyana to the north of the city. Only a decisive intervention by the French cavalry saved the bridge and forced the Spanish to withdraw to the city. In July the hot summer temperatures reduced activities during some weeks, but by the middle of August the Spanish renewed their attacks. This time the objective was not the lines of circumvallation, nor the bridges, but the main quarters of

---

46 The garrison of Lleida was a mix of soldiers (Spanish, Walloons and Germans) defeated at San Lorenz the previous year, and new recruits with no experience.

47 See section 2.2.3 above.
48 In June and July new infantry regiments, arrived to reinforce the army of Harcourt, bringing probably, some 5,000 men. The regiments were: Guyenne, Gesvres, Roquelaure, Vaillac, Nerestang and Lorraine.

Harcourt, the Quarter of the King. The Spanish launched a series of small attacks by night to create confusion, killing French soldiers, but also, where possible, taking fresh meat and fish from French supplies. If conditions were appalling in the French lines, the soldiers and citizens in Lleida suffered additionally from hunger and a lack of fresh food. Civilians had to pay for food and by the beginning of September money was scare. Brito wanted to reserve as much food as possible for the soldiers so as to keep control of the city. A row broke out between Brito and the civilian authorities and finally Brito agreed to give food to the people, but the cost was the expulsion of 300 civilians from the city in October.[49] All these drastic and dramatic measures had only one goal, to retain as much of the supplies as possible for the exclusive use of the Spanish soldiers – Lleida was a vital strategic position.

By the middle of September, four months after the last convoy had entered Lleida, Harcourt was determined to continue the siege behind his fortified lines, and Brito was equally determined to keep Lleida at any price. The main movement occurred between Fraga and Monzon on the river Cinca. The Spanish commander, the Marques of Léganez, had managed to organise a powerful army, beginning with 6,000 Foot (16 tercios and regiments) and 3,400 Horse, raising it up to 12,000 infantry (18 Spanish tercios[50] and 8

tercios/regiments[51] from the nations) and 3,500 cavalry by the end of September. With an army of 15,500 men,[52] the Spanish were more confident of challenging the French, much reduced after five months of operations against Lleida. However, a military operation to relieve Lleida was not one without its problems. By the end of September, the Spanish received a detailed report on the French positions around Lleida, their strengths and weaknesses, as well as the military state of the region of Lleida and the Urgell valley. To summarise, the Spanish had two main options: the first was to march towards Lleida and to attack the well-defended French lines; the second option, preferred by the governor of Lleida, was to capture the French rearguard positions, especially Cervera, in order to cut Harcourt's supply lines to Barcelona. Both options had advantages and drawbacks: the first was highly risky if Harcourt concentrated his army; the second meant that the Spanish would have to operate for several weeks away from their main base, the city of Fraga, in a devastated area, and where supplies would have to come from Tarragona. This option implied that if the army was not well supplied it could melt away through illness and desertion. No formal decision was taken when the army went out from Fraga on 30th September. After four days the army was in front of Torre de Segre. Here the Spanish built a bridge and Léganes decided to install a strong garrison of 4,000 men, the rest advanced to Sudanell. On 5th October a reconaissance of the French lines was carried out by the main officers, protected by 2,000

---

[49] The controversial attitude of the governor can be found in different Spanish sources such as Catalán [1919].

[50] Eight regular Spanish tercios (Tercio of Guardia del Rey [Maestro de Campo, Pablo de Parada], Tercio of Alonso Villamayor, Tercio of Diego de Villalva, Tercio of Luis de Silva, Tercio of Liboa [Maestro de Campo, Diego de Aguilera], Tercio of Juan de Garcés, Tercio of the Marques o Lorenzana and Tercio of Cristóbal Salgado), one tercio of Tortosa (formed by the garrison of Tortosa, commanded by Francisco de Soto), four provincial tercios from Aragón (Tercio Viejo of Zaragoza, commanded by the Mayor Sergent, Tomas Dezal), one provincial tercio from Navarra (commanded by Josef Beaumonte), one provincial tercio from Castilla (commanded by the Count of Baños), three tercios extracted from the armada (Tercio de Galeones – commanded by Rodrigo Niño de Mendoza, Tercio of Luis de Sotomayor and Tercio of Benevides).

[51] Two Walloon tercios (Tercio of Charles Antoine de Calonne and Tercio of the Baron of Van der Straeten), four Italian tercios (Tercio of Scipio Pignatiello, Tercio of the Prince of San Felices, Tercio of the Baron of Amato and Tercio of Fray Pietro Brancaccio) and two German regiments (the Regiment of the Baron of Seebach and the Regiment of the Count of Grosfeilt). We can also add the two Irish tercios of James Preston and Patrick Fitzgerald with few men.

[52] The figure of 15,500 men does not include the fifer's, drummers, chaplain and ensigns of each infantry company, as well as the staff of each tercio, regiment and cavalry trozo. We should therefore increase the strength by some 1,500 men. Pradet in *Memorial Historico* T24, gives 14,000 Foot and 4,000 Horse.

Horse. French squadrons, under Balthazar, came out of the fortifications and a large skirmish took place, with both sides claiming victory.

The reconnaissance report reached Spanish headquarters during the night, and the news was not good: the French fortifications were stronger than expected, and worst, the French soldiers were alert and prepared to receive an attack. In the subsequent war council most of the Spanish commanders acknowledged that a frontal attack would be suicidal so they decided to apply the more indirect strategy, cutting Harcourt supply lines. With 12,000–13,000 men, Léganes moved and took Les Borges Blanques without resistance. From here small villages, such as Castelldans and Arbeca,[53] were also taken after some fighting against Catalans from the *somaten*. Leaving troops to garrison the area, the Spanish next moved to take Bellpuig where they encountered little resistance from the 300–400 French soldiers fortified in the castle. The next step was Tarrega, also taken without much resistance on 14th October. In Tarrega, Léganes installed his headquarters and the core of his army, just 11 km from Cervera, which was defended by a strong French garrison. From here, he launched a column consisting of the Tercios of Galleon and of Villalva against Agramunt; the town was taken without difficulty. At the same time, Tuttavila was sent south with a strong column of 2,000 men to protect a Spanish convoy coming from Tarragona with supplies. On the French side, Harcourt did not have an army large enough to both properly guard the 26 km long lines of circumvallation and to challenge Léganez in Tarrega. Drawing men from the Catalan and French regiments located near Barcelona and Girona, the Catalan commander Margarit managed to strongly reinforce the garrison of Cervera, raising it to around 4,000 men in total. Faced with a well-defended city,

Léganez decided to attack Pons to the north in order to close the lines of communication to Harcourt. In Pons the French and Catalans had a garrison of 800–1,000 men with a lot of supplies. For the operation against Pons, Leganes detached a force of seven tercios (Tercios of de la Guardia, de Villamayor, Zaragoza, Van der Straeten and the three tercios of Aragon), supported by 400 Horse under the command of Tuttavilla. The Spanish launched a direct attack, capturing the city and the garrison after few hours of combat.

With the French lines of communication cut, the Spanish managed to capture small convoys so Harcourt ordered larger convoys prepared. The first one was organised at the end of October at Cervera; with a strong escort it managed to elude Spanish patrols, and when it was finally discovered, the local Spanish commander did not have sufficient strength to challenge it. On 30th October it entered the French camp at Vilanoveta. A second convoy was organised at Montblanc and again managed to pass though Spanish lines. Finally, a third convoy set out from Balaguer, the supply depot, and also managed to reach French lines. The Spanish strategy of cutting French supply lines had clearly failed, Harcourt probably had supplies for more than four weeks, whilst the Spanish army was running short in this devastated country.[54] On 16th November, Léganes was in Bellpuig with a portion of the army, he sent letters to all the Spanish commanders to explain his plan; the idea was to launch a double attack on the French lines. The main attack would be against the core of the French forces in the lines facing the village of Albatàrrec, while a second attack, with supplies for the beleaguered city, would be launched to the north-west of the King's Quarter. The main forces would join together at Sudanell on 18th November, while the Baron of Bouthier organised a detachment with the Cavalry of Burgundy and infantry from the garrison of Fraga. On 19th Novem-

53 In Arbeca, the Spanish encountered Spanish prisoners, including Maestro de Campo Diego de Toledo, Mayor Sergent Florencia and Captain Juan de Sarabia from the Tercio of la Guardia, taken prisoner on 23rd June when the garrison of Lleida launched the attack against the north bridge.

54 In face of the Spanish advance, the French cavalry applied a sort of "terre brulée" tactic destroying all the windmill and stored grain of the area, and burning what they could not transport.

ber, the Duke of Infantado arrived at Sudanell with 1,000 Horse and six tercios. He was joined late afternoon by Léganes with another 1,000 Horse, the rest of the infantry, and the artillery. In total, in Sudanell, the Marques of Léganes had only 2,000 Horse and less than 5,500 Foot. The rest of the 16,000–17,000 men were in garrisons between Bellpuig and Torres de Segre, in hospitals unfit for active service, dead, or had just deserted. Immediately the Spanish started to build a bridge on the river Segre to send the baggage back. The first idea was to attack the following night but heavy rains started on the night of the 19th and the attack had to be postponed. Meanwhile the French were watching the Spanish movements; Harcourt and the French officers were convinced that Léganes was trying to withdraw to Fraga. This impression was reinforced when the army of Léganes started moving in the direction of the village of Alfés on the morning of 21st November. For the French soldiers the vision of the Spanish retiring to the west was a comfortable one, the tension of the previous days reduced, finally no heavy fighting would take place and the city would not be rescued. For the garrison of Lleida and the inhabitants of the city the vision was distressful, only Gregorio of Brito knew that Léganes would attack soon. By 1 p.m. the Spanish army halted and the main commanders of the army began to organise it for battle, the joy of the soldiers was immense – the time of marching was over, the reputation of the army would be put to the test by fighting the French. The army was organised into two brigades. The vanguard (seven squadrons and five battalions) under Francisco Tuttavilla had three Spanish battalions in the centre, from right to left:

- Battalion 1 formed by the Tercio of the Guardia del rey, the Tercio of the Galeones and the Tercio of Navarra;[55]
- Battalion 2 formed by the Tercio of Alonso Villamayor and the Tercio Viejo of the City of Zaragoza;

- Battalion 3 formed by the Tercio of Villalva and some Irish companies from the Tercio of Fitzgerald.

The first line was flanked by two cavalry squadrons with respectively 150 and 100 Horse. The second line was formed by a strong battalion formed by three tercios raised by Aragon and two cavalry squadrons under the command of Don Carlos de Padilla. On the extreme left there was a fifth battalion formed by the two tercios of Walloons (Tercio of Calonne and Tercio of Van der Straeten). Between the two lines was the Duke of Infantado with two cavalry squadrons. To complete the deployment of the vanguard Tuttavila dispatched a small detachment, under Don Lorenzo Salazar, with a *manga* of 120 musketeers from the Tercio Viejo of Zaragoza and a cavalry squadron of 150 Horse, to demonstrate in front of Vilanoveta, making a lot of noise and trying to attract the attention of the French commanders. The vanguard was also supported by two batteries of four guns (six-pounders) under the command of Tiberio Brancaccio. Behind the vanguard came the battaille, under the command of Léganes, with probably six to seven squadrons of cavalry (Company of Guards, Company of Volunteers, Trozo of the Ordenes and Guards of Castilla), probably three Spanish battalions (formed by the Tercio Viejo de Lisboa, Tercio of Silva, Tercio of Lorenzana, Tercio of Salgado, Tercio of Garcés), one amalgamated German battalion (Regiment of the Baron of Seebach, Regiment of Grosfeit) and probably one amalgamated Italian battalion (Tercios of Pignatello and San Felices). If the detachment of the Baron of Bouthier is taken into account, the Spanish were attacking the French lines with only 2,500 cavalry (16-17 squadrons), 6,000 infantry (11 battalions) and 8 light guns.

On the other side of the siege lines, the order of battle of the French army is difficult to establish. As mentioned previously, the Count of Harcourt began the siege of Lleida in May with some 12,000 Foot and 5,500 Horse. In June and October, Harcourt received reinforcements of infantry and cavalry. Unfortunately for the French, operations around Lleida took place in a difficult

---

[55] Some Spanish sources place the Tercio of Navarra in the bataille.

environment, during a hot summer, with little or no rain, restrictions on food supply, numerous desertions, illness and increasing casualties. Also, numerous detachments were sent back to cover Cervera and Flix. An estimation of the French force inside the lines of circumvallation would be 3,500–4,000 Horse and some 8,000 Foot, reinforced by 900-1,000 Catalans, in total less than 13,000 men. Compared with Spanish forces it would give them a significant superiority if Harcourt could concentrate them in the right place. In his numerous books, Susane gives a good estimation of the French regiments present at the siege of Lleida. There is a list of 18 French infantry regiments (Champagne, Entragues, Harcourt, Rébé, Gesvre, Vaillac, Ferrières, Mirepoix, Monpouillan, Le Ferron, Saintonge, Montpeyron, Mérinville-Infanterie, Eperon, Couvonges, Sainte Mesme, Roquelaure and La Marine) and the Swiss regiment of Colonel Nicolas Rhoom. With the reinforcement for the cavalry we find a company of guards, a the company of gendarmes for Harcourt, and a list of 15 cavalry regiments (Le Ferron-Cavalerie, Balthazard, Mérinville-Cavalerie, Gesyres, Terrail, Boissac, Châteaubriant, Lorraine, Bougy, de la Mothe-Houdancourt. Harcourt, Alais, Bentivoglio, Gaut-Italien and Mazarin-Italien). The Catalan contingent consisted of one battalion from the Tercio of Barcelona with 600 men (Tercio commanded by Jéronimo Tamarit), four companies from the region of Girona, and a horse company incorporated into the Regiment of Alais. The selected point of attack was covered by Fort Rébé and two other smaller forts, one covering a bridge on the river Segre, connecting the quarter of Couvonges, and the other one in between, called the Fort of Grau Alemany. The forts were joined by the line of circumvallation, covering the quarter of Chateaubriand. The troops guarding the line were from the Regiment of the Baron of Rébé, the Regiment of Champagne (commanded by the Baron of Origny) and the Battalion of Barcelona, they were supported by six to eight light guns.

As we have seen, the Spanish vanguard was marching toward the French lines under a strong wind and by 10 p.m. they were less than a kilometre from Fort Rébé. Here the Spanish soldiers waited silently, the hour of the attack was fixed by the council of war at 5 a.m. on 22nd November. Some minutes later, two gunshots were heard, it was a signal from French officers to indicate Spanish movement and that reinforcements from the quarter of Couvonges were needed. Thinking that the surprise was discovered, the Marques of Léganes advanced the hour of the attack and by 10.40 a.m. the Spanish were just a few hundred metres from the French position. The attack on Fort Rébé was executed by two columns: Battalion 1 in the centre and Battalions 2 and 3 on the left, looking towards the city. With scaling ladders and fascines, the Spanish soldiers entered Fort Rébé, defended only by 30 to 50 men;[56] it took only a few minutes for the defences to be neutralised and the fortification taken. Supposedly the first man to enter the fort was Matias Cacho, a captain of the Regiment de la Guardia del rey. On the left, Battalion 2 was the first to take the east gate of the fort and to take position to repulse the incoming French soldiers of the Regiment of Champagne. The Baron of Origny quickly grasped that the Spanish had launched a strong attack on the French position and when the first French soldiers of his regiment withdrew, he realised that he needed to form an improvised defensive position. When the Spanish battalions advanced, a bitter fight started, but the French had to give ground and when Origny was killed, they slowly retired to Vilanoveta. Meantime, further to the north, the third attack commenced, conducted by Charles Calonne with the Walloons against the Fort of Grau Alemany, defended by soldiers from the battalion of Barcelona. In a few minutes the Catalan battalion was destroyed, losing in the fighting their Mayor Sergeant, four captains and many soldiers, the rest fled toward

---

[56] Normally Fort Rébé had a garrison of 300 men, which could be expanded up to 500 men. But with all the movements of the previous days, and the bad weather, attention had been focused elsewhere and only a few guards were to be found in the fort at the moment of the attack.

Vilanoveta. Calonne reorganised the position to face a probable counter-attack.

For the Spanish, the tactical surprise had worked completely and most of the infantry were now destroying the palisades and filling in the trench with fascines in order to prepare the terrain for the cavalry. The first part of the plan was a complete success, Harcourt, now awake to the realisation that he had nothing to fear from the musket fire of the small detachment of Don Lorenzo Salazar, sent orders to all French quarters to join him at Vilanoveta. After the initial attack, the orders given to Francisco Tuttavilla were to organise a powerful defensive position between Fort Rébé and the Fort of Grau Alemany in order to meet the French counterattack. For some reason, the Duke of Infantado started to advance in pursuit the French from the Regiment of Champagne, Tuttavila supported this action with two battalions (Battalions 2 and 3). At first, with 800 Horse and 900 Foot, the Duke of Infantado was able to harass the French retiring on Vilanoveta, but at a few hundred metres from the village, Harcourt was waiting with the elite of his cavalry and several French infantry and cavalry regiments. With a clear superiority over the incoming Spanish, the French cavalry charged three times and at the third attempt forced the Spanish to retire. Left alone, the infantry made a brief stand before retreating in considerable disorder. Most of the casualties of this defeat were taken by the cavalry and officers of the infantry, including the Maestro de Campo Villalva, three sergeant mayors, and several captains. Fortunately for the Spanish, most of the soldiers managed to reach the safety of Fort Rébé, albeit in complete disorder; it was midnight. Here, Pablo de Parada, and the Sergeant Mayor of the Tercio of Zaragoza decided to resist and organised a strong defensive position with 1,000 men. On the ramp accessing the fort they placed a strong squadron with all the pikes available gathered behind a barricade and covered by *mangas* of harquebusiers, while *mangas* of musketeers and two light guns were placed in the small bastions protecting access to the fort. The rest of the men were sent to the rear

to be reorganised. To the north, the Baron of Couvonges managed to cross the river Segre with three French regiments. Using the confusion of the Spanish, they expelled the Walloons of Calonne from their position, retaking the Fort of Grau Alemany. Couvonges next intended to attack the troops in Fort Rébé from the north but they were stopped in-extremis by the reorganised cavalry of the Duke of Infantado and had to retire on Grau Alemany where they commenced an annoying flanking fire on the Spanish positions to the south.

The critical point of the battle arrived when Harcourt emerged from the shadows of the night with his cavalry regiment, gendarmes and guards, followed by the rest of his troops. The first charge was executed by the elite cavalry, but when they were 50 metres from the barricades, they were met by a terrible fire from the musketeers and harquebusiers. The disrupted French squadrons were easily repulsed by the pikemen. Another charge was launched with similar results. The problem facing the French was threefold: the ramp had a narrow width and only a squadron of 150 Horse could charge over it; the darkness of the night made visibility of the battlefield very poor; the French infantry had no scaling ladders. On the Spanish side, Pablo de Parada sent a messenger to the rear to give an accurate report of the situation and to ask for reinforcements. Near Albatàrrec, the Marques of Léganes was anxious; he had learnt that after the successful attack on Fort Rébé, the Spanish troops had been beaten. Fugitives from the battlefield had given terrifying reports from the front line and the details of what was happening were confused. Léganes' first thought was to cover the retreat of the vanguard and then to withdraw to Fraga, consequently he sent messages to Parada to retire. But when the messenger sent by Parada arrived, he reconsidered the situation and gave orders to send reinforcements to the vanguard to hold the position of Fort Rébé and to retake the position of Grau Alemany. With this reinforcement, the Duke of Infantado retook the initiative and attacked the troops of Couvonges. After a short fight the French were expelled again and had to withdraw behind the river Segre, the Spanish had secured the position again. At Fort Rébé, Harcourt was launching assault after assault with all the troops he had to hand. Every time they were met by Spanish musket volleys and the casualties mounted. Harcourt became obsessed by the fort and for three hours the French soldiers attacked the Spanish positions without success. In the fort, Pablo Parada and Francisco Tuttavila refreshed their forces with the reinforcements from Léganes in order to hold the position. At 4 a.m. it was evident that the French could not retake Fort Rébé, Harcourt ordered a last suicidal attack, but this was blocked by his officers. When he recovered his calm, Harcourt ordered a withdrawal to the quarter of Vilanoveta. Harcourt's plan was now to again engage the Spanish advancing across the plain where his cavalry was still superior to theirs. Unfortunately for him, at 3:30 a.m., he received news of a new Spanish attack, the Baron of Bouthier had finally entered the action. According to the original plan, Bouthier had attacked the French circumvallation lines to the north-west of the quarter of the king, on the road to Alpicat. At 3 a.m., 400 Horse and 400 Foot from Bouthier's force breached the French position, meeting little resistance. Immediately, the rest of Bouthier's detachment, with the 300 mules, advanced toward the city of Lleida. At 4 a.m., the 1,100 men of Bouthier's force were inside Lleida, the first reinforcement for Brito since 12th May. Rapidly the news of the entrance of Bouthier into Lleida spread around the French positions and among the French units in Vilanoveta. The French officers and soldiers had no clear information concerning the size of Bouthier's force, they only understood that a Spanish force with Horse and Foot had arrived in Lleida and that they could threaten their withdrawal to Balaguer. Like a sugar cube dropped into water, the French started to melt away, initially in an orderly manner, towards the northern bridge of Grenyana. But, with false rumours spreading among the French soldiers and the heavy losses suffered during the night, the retreat degenerated in a frenetic race to cross the river Segre.

Meanwhile, the Spanish located in Fort Rébé stood awaiting another attack from the French. Finally Léganes ordered the Duke of Infantado to move cautiously to Vilanoveta. At the same time the cavalry of Bouthier was also slowly crossing the main bridge of Lleida. The slow movement of the Spanish cavalry gave Harcourt time to save most of his men, only 350 were taken prisoners, but the artillery (22 guns and 14 light guns) and a large proportion of the baggage had to be abandoned. The next day, the French garrison of the castle of Alguaire was captured. Harcourt had suffered a terrible defeat; in 36 hours the French had lost some 500 dead, 2,000 wounded (some of which would die in the following days and weeks) and up to 750 prisoners. For the Spanish, the victory had cost some 420 men, 100 dead and up to 320 wounded, including 8 senior officers (4 Maestros de campo and 4 Sergeants Mayor). By the end of November, the Marques of Léganes reinforced the garrison of Lleida and sent back the remainder of his troops, including those in Bellpuig and Torres de Segre, to winter quarters. Harcourt reinforced the garrison of Ballaguer with 2,000 men and returned to Barcelona with the remains of his army. Harcourt's disaster was a terrible blow for the French minister Mazarin. It arrived after the failure of the operation in Tuscany;[57] discontent was increasing, not only among the French population but also among a proportion of the nobility. In December 1646, Mazarin dismissed the Count of Harcourt and managed to convince Louis II of Bourbon, Prince of Condé,[58] to become the

---

[57] The expedition of Orbetello took place between May and July 1646. After a successful landing of 9,000 men the French began operations against Orbetello. The Spanish reacted by sending a fleet and an army from Naples, commanded by the Duke of Arcos. The naval battle fought from 14th to 16th June ended in a draw. The fortress was relieved at the end of July by the army of the duke of Arcos.

[58] Louis II of Bourbon was born on 8th September 1621 in Saint Germain (France) and died 11th November 1686 in Chantilly (France). He was Duke of Enghien until 1646 and became the fourth Prince of Condé on 26th December 1646, he was a *prince de sang*. Louis of Bourbon was one of the best French generals of the 17th century and was nicknamed *le Grand Condé*.

next viceroy of Catalonia and to restore the prestige of the French monarchy again.

3.5 The 1647 Campaign: The Third Siege of Lleida

At the beginning of the year the Prince of Condé and the main French commanders were discussing the best strategy for the year. Condé had high political aspirations and for that he wanted a quick victory so that he could return to Paris as soon as possible and with glory. Like the previous year, two possible options were to besiege one of the main Spanish positions, Tarragona or Lleida. A third and fourth option was to attack the reserve fortresses, Fraga for Lleida, and Tortosa for Tarragona. The option of attacking Lleida was chosen, for different reasons: the excellent strategic position of the city, most of the circumvallation lines were still intact, and the Spanish were not expecting another attack on that front. Condé did not want to conduct a similar siege as that made by Harcourt, he had no time to loose and he wanted a quick victory.

For the Spanish the situation was far from ideal; the first task of the new Spanish Captain General of Catalonia, the Marques of Aytona, was to provide adequate garrisons for Fraga, Lleida, Tarragona and Tortosa, as well as the cities on the river Cinca. The second task was to build a field army, but for that he needed the tercios from the Armada, the militia from Aragon, Valencia and Navarra, and new recruits for the Castellan tercios. The problem for Aytona was that to raise a field army would take time and time was just what Condé did not want to give him. Another problem was discovered in April 1647 when the paymaster[59] of the Army of Catalonia was arrested and accused of having falsified the accounts of the garrisons

of Lleida and Fraga. Following the payment made at the beginning of the year, the garrison of Lleida was supposed to have 4,000 men, but the real number was closer to 2,600.

The Prince of Condé arrived in Barcelona on 11th April. He had been preceded by the arrival of numerous troops to compensate for the losses suffered the previous year.[60] He used the prestige and reputation of his name to expand his field army in Barcelona. On 22nd April, with the arrival of the regiments[61] of the house of Condé, he had an army of 10,000 infantry and 4,000 cavalry. With Condé new faces also arrived: the Marshal of Gramont, Lieutenant General Marsin, La Moussaye, and above all the engineer François de la Valière. Gregorio de Brito was still the governor of Lleida, he had little time and money to achieve all the necessary repairs before the arrival of Condé. At the beginning of May Brito had 2,842 Foot[62] and 505 Horse. Following Gonzalo et al. (1991) the artillery of the city of Lleida consisted of one full-cannon of 45 pounds (with 88 cannonballs), 3 half-cannon of 20 pounds (with 1,337 cannonballs), 10 quarter-cannon of 10 and 12 pounds (with 4,002 cannonballs), the rest being 18 lighter guns (Sacres, Mansfelts and falconets) of 1.5 to 6 pounds. In the Castle of Gardenny, the Spanish had 9 guns, 1 half-cannon, 5 quarter-cannon, 2 sacres of 4 pounds and 1 falconet of 1.5 pounds.

On 6th May a spy indicated to the Spanish that the city of Cervera was full of

---

[59] Don Juan de Aguirre, the paymaster of Lleida, was responsible of the review of the garrison of Lleida and was sending the correct number to Don Antonio de la Torre Barreda. By some tricks of accountancy, the number sent to Madrid was increased to 4,000 men and the government of Mardrid was giving the money to Barreda. This typical case of corruption had consequence for the ability of the Spanish to maintain Lleida.

[60] Following Gonzalo et al. [1991], before the arrival of the reinforcement of Condé, the French Army of Catalonia was reduced to 4,000 Foot and 1,500 Horse.

[61] The house of Condé maintained four infantry regiments: Condé, Enghien, Persans and Conti. The cavalry was formed by his Company of Guards, the Company of Gendarmes, and the regiment of Enghien-Cavalerie, later Condé-Cavalerie. In April 1647 they numbered in total, up to 4,000 men.

[62] The garrison of Lleida consisted of: 352 men from the Tercio de la Guardia, 412 from the Tercio of Pedro Osteriz, 398 men from the Tercio of Galeones, 439 men from the Tercio of the Count of Aguilar, 170 men from the Regiment of Ludwig Haumel, 412 men from the companies of the Castle of Lleida; in total 2,142 men in 79 companies supported by 700 men from the militia of Lleida. The cavalry was formed by 13 companies totalling 505 men.

supplies for the siege and that between Agramunt and Cervera, the French had only 300 cavalry and 300 infantry, with the support of 200 Catalans. With the authorisation of Aytona, Brito decided to go to Cervera and destroy all the supplies he could. On 9th May Brito received reinforce-ment from Fraga and with 1,500 infantry and all the cavalry, he went directly to Cervera. Unfortunately for the Spanish, the information proved false, in fact the spy was working for the French and when Brito arrived near Cervera, the Spanish scouts found that most of the French army was waiting for them. Brito immediately understood the magnitude of the trap and he ordered a retreat to Lleida as quickly as possible. In a frenetic race the Spanish managed to reach the city, losing only few men in the process.

Three days later, 13,000 Frenchmen were in front of Lleida, occupying the old quarters of Harcourt from the previous year. At that time the roads were difficult and the heavy artillery train of Condé[63] took more than 10 days to arrive at this destination. During this time the only fighting took place on 20th May when hundreds of French soldiers were isolated by the destruction of one of the boat-bridges on the river Segre. The Spanish governor took advantage of the opportunity and sent 200 Foot with some Horse to attack positions near the quarter of Vilanoveta. The attack was a total success and the French lost some 150–200 men in dead, wounded and prisoners. Finally, on 25th May, Condé had all his artillery, the lines of circumvallation were finished, and the bridge repaired. According to a letter sent by Brito to the Marques of Aytona at the beginning of June,[64] on 27th May 1647 the

French had in front of Lleida some 8,200 Foot, 4,900 Horse and 500 volunteers, distributed into six quarters. In a council of war he explained his strategy, the city would be attacked directly and the point of attack would be the new fortress of Lleida on the top of the hill. The location of the attack was a surprise for Brito as he was expecting the main effort more to the west, directly at the city, between the gate of San Martin and the gate of San Antonio. It is possible that a direct line of attack on the wall of the city would end with success, but while the fortress was in Spanish hands, Condé could not claim victory, so the plan was to directly take the main Spanish position using their superior artillery and mining. Also, as we said before, Condé had little time to expend on the capture of Lleida, he did not want to face the Spanish field army while he was besieging the city and he expected to take it in a matter of weeks.

On the night of 27th May the French started to work on the approach trenches to establish positions for the heavy guns. The next day a first battery of five guns was operational and opened a terrible fire on the gates of the Infantes. In a matter of hours, the gate was mostly destroyed and a small breach was opened. Brito immediately sent men from the Tercio of Osteriz to reinforce the position. Osteriz and his men managed to save the position and during the night conducted a successful attack on the French position with little loss to themselves. On 30th May a new battery of five guns was in position more to the west and the miners under the engineers de la Vallieres and de la Pomme were advancing inexorably from the convent of San Juan to the foundations of the wall of the fortress.

Meantime, the French, under Marschal of Gramont, were moving to another point, to the west of the Gate of the Infantes to attack the fortress. The first step was to take the ruins of the convent of San Francisco, an outpost defended by one sergeant and twelve musketeers. Some 800 men from the Regiment of Persan and the Regiment of

---

[63] The Prince of Condé had a powerful artillery train made of 35 cannon and half cannon, and an undetermined numbers of lighter guns.

[64] Campaña de 1647, CODOIN nº95. The infantry was divided into 11 French regiments (Champagne, Nerestang, Condé, Conti, Persan, Enghien, Guyenne, Lorraine, Périgord, Albret and la Vallière) and 3 Swiss regiments (Rhoom, Praroman and Rhan). The Horse was divided into 4 companies of Guards and Gendarmes (Chevaux Léger of Condé, Gendarmes of Condé, Guards of Condé and Guards of Gramont) and

---

17 Cavalry regiments. The cavalry was reinforced by 500 volunteers from the French nobility (see Table 3).

Lorraine advanced, but even after three hours of fighting they could not subdue the defence, which was supported by the artillery of Lleida. On 2nd June, the French prepared a full-scale attack with two guns and a mine. In the early morning of the 3rd June the mine exploded, killing six of the Spaniards and probably a dozen French. Another three Spaniards were captured and the other four managed to escape to the city. The capture of the convent was complete, but for the French it was a bitter victory as the heroic defence of a dozen men had halted the French for two full days. Quickly, Condé installed a battery of seven guns in front of the convent. Now the French general had two lines of approaches: the attack of Condé west of the Gate of the Infantes, and the attack of Gramont in front of the convent of San Francisco. On 2nd June, during intense fighting to the west, François de la Vallière received a mortal wound from a musket ball, dying the next day. The death of la Vallière and the slow progress of his mine pushed Condé to focus more on the other attack. In two days he strongly reinforced the attack of Gramont with more guns. On 4th June, the French had up to 30 guns (7 batteries) of 24 to 45 pounders at only 200–300 metres from the fortress. The same day Monsieur du Plessis arrived with a reinforcement of 6,000 infantry[65] and 1,500 cavalry. For Brito, the lack of men to cover all positions meant that he had to optimise his forces. He moved half of the garrison of the Guardeny to reinforce the front of the Bastion of Cantelmo. He also organised a crack company of 100 men with his best soldiers and officers, the company of the red scarf, armed with halberds, *chuzos* and pistols. Brito also noticed that the rapid approach of the French meant that their trenches were not well defended. He decided to organise an attack the same night. Sallying out from the Gate of the Infantes with 100 Horse and 200 Foot, Captain Antonio de Palacio managed to reach the French trenches, killing all the guards. They set fire to the wooden works, destroying everything before retiring with little loss. The next morning the French could see the disaster, but Condé was one of the best generals of the 17th century. In a matter of hours, the trenches were rebuilt and garrisoned with more soldiers. Inside the city, Brito was concerned about the mines prepared by the French, he convinced the inhabitants of Lleida to prepare three countermines. Until now all of Brito's actions have been undertaken at night and the French were forced to maintain a strong garrison in the dark. The Spanish governor decided to switch tactics and at midday on 6th June a strong force of 400 Spanish went out from the gate of San Martin and fell upon the Swiss regiments guarding the position. After a brief fight, the Swiss abandoned their post and a select number of Spaniards entered the French mines, killing all the miners inside, including Monsieur de la Pomme. In this action the French lost 400 men and the Spanish less than 40. The next day, Condé gathered 3,000 men for a formal attack on the Spanish fortress to test the Spanish defences. Different columns of French infantry went up but they met strong resistance and had to retire to their starting position, this time losses were heavy in both camps. Over the next two days, the French again worked on the mines and the Spanish conducted small attacks during the night. On 9th June the Spanish fired homemade grenades into the French trenches with success. On the morning of the 10th, Marshal Gramont sent an emissary to Brito to organise a truce of six hours to remove a decomposing cadaver located on the slope of the hill. For good psychological reasons, but against the spirit of the time, Brito argued that for reasons of protocol it was impossible to do so. The Spanish officer judged correctly that the morale of the French soldiers was suffering due to the difficulties of the siege, the high casualty rate, the hot weather, and that the cadavers were more a problem for the French than for the Spanish. But the prince of Condé was not a common general, and his obstinacy and the heavy gun fire was destroying, piece

---

[65] Probably from the ten French regiments (Vaillac, Mirepoix, Monpouillan, Saint Aumetz, Le Ferron, Marchin, Rébé, La Marine, Montpeyroux and Mérinville-Infanterie) and two Catalan regiments (Marguerit and Aragó). This list was taken from General Susane, *Histoire de l'Infanterie Française*.

by piece, the wall of the Spanish fortress. By 10th June, the wall already had three breaches of 60 to 80 metres, but this was still not enough to launch a massive attack. Inside the fortress, Brito was rotating his men in order to always have fresh men ready to receive the French. On 11th June the Spanish again attacked the French trenches, this time guarded by the Regiment of Montpouillan. This time Condé sent Monsieur de Saint Martin with the Regiment of Champagne and others troops to counterattack. The French position was retaken after fierce fighting, but the French again lost 300–400 men to 30–40 for the Spanish. Condé was forced to take drastic measures to boost the morale of his troops, sending 400 dismounted cavalry into the trenches. Unfortunately for the French, even if their guns were breaching Spanish walls, the Spanish had also installed 10 quarter-cannon and they fired continuously on the French trenches full of soldiers, causing substantial casualties. By now the siege was a question of will, Condé had news that a powerful army was assembling in Fraga – he had no time to lose. On 13th June, Brito launched his most risky operation against the French positions; 100 dismounted cavalry and 100 men of the red scarf company managed to occupy part of the position for 90 minutes, destroying all they could. These time losses were more equal, the Spanish suffered 60 casualties, including Brito, who was wounded in the operation. From that day, Condé and his men were better at defending their trenches against the attacks of the garrison, but each night small skirmishes were taking place. For the Spanish the situation was becoming more problematic as the French mines were advancing each day. On 17th June, the Spanish were expecting the explosion of a mine at any moment, but nothing happened. The next day a surprised garrison saw the French soldiers withdrawing their heavy guns. Brito could not believe it, Condé was abandoning the siege and the garrison of Lleida had won a victory against one of the best French generals, losing only 300–400 men.

So what happened? If we go back to 16th June, Gramont and Condé had judged that the situation was not good at all. The

miners had found the hard stone difficult to dig, and even if they were close to the wall, it would take weeks to be under the wall. Also losses among the miners and engineers had been particularly heavy during the last three weeks. The morale of the French was low, and losses had been significant over the last seven weeks. Gonzalo et al (1991) estimated the French losses at a minimum of 3,000 dead and wounded and probably 5,000 deserters, mainly in the infantry. Other sources increase these numbers up to 5,000 dead and wounded and 4,000 deserters; Condé had lost between 7,000 and 9,000 men. On 17th June Condé probably had 13,500 men (6,000 Horse and 7,500 Foot) around Lleida, but he considered this number insufficient to defend the 26 km of circumvallation lines, as well as to continue the attack on the Spanish fortress. Furthermore, Condé did not really trust his army. The 35 days of the siege had been very hard for the French soldiers in the trenches, excluding the high losses; the Spanish governor used all his skill to conduct a form of physiological warfare. According to one story, Brito and the French had an agreement to let a servant pass with iced fruit juices or ice water with lemon every afternoon for the Prince of Condé. For Gramont it was a symbol of deference for a prince of royal blood, but for the poor infantryman, fighting, digging in the trenches in a hot weather and smelling the odour of their dead comrades, the vision of a glass of fresh water could be disturbing and demoralizing. Another story was that some of the French soldiers were saying that during the night, Brito changed into a wolf or spirit to spy on them and later to attack them at their weak point. In fact Brito did not need any magic tricks, the French camp was full of Spanish spies and the Spanish governor had enough money to entice them. Whatever the real reason was, on 19th June, the Prince of Condé was in Balaguer crossing the river and the Marques of Mortara was entering the city of Lleida with supplies, money and a reinforcement of 1,000 men.[66] The Prince of Condé moved his

---

[66] This reinforcement was formed of 300 Spanish to reinforce the existing tercios, the rest being from the

army to between the Borges Blanques and Arbeca on 28th June, where he established a powerful camp to rebuild a coherent army. From there, he could still be a threat against Tarragona, Tortosa or even Lleida – he was just 15 km south of the city. He also reinforced the garrisons of Balaguer, Flix and Cervera, as well as the positions of Salou and Constanti in the camp of Tarragona.

On the Spanish side the Marques of Aytona had an army of 10,000 Foot[67] and 3,200 Horse, but he received news that the French were well entrenched only 15–18 km from Lleida. Aytona received an order from the Spanish council to reinforce the garrison of Lleida, to send money to repair the walls, and to destroy the French trenches around the city and to send back 1,000 men to Tarragona and Tortosa. With a hot summer's day, Aytona went back to Fraga with the rest of the army. Lastly, Juan de Austria's armada of 50 ships received an order to maintain themselves at full alert between Denia and Vinaroz to prevent any French movement against Tarragona. The two armies remained in their quarters all summer. After two months in Borgues Blanques, the Prince of Condé moved his army to the east, closer to Cervera, to a place called Verdu. The two armies were waking up, the Marques of Aytona in Fraga had now gathered an army of 11,000–12,000 men and Condé, with the reinforcement of 1,500 recruits, probably had some 10,000 men. The first to move was the French general; he crossed the Segre at Balaguer and established his army at Castelló de Farfanya. From there he selected a force of 2,400 Foot and 400 Horse, supported by two guns, and marched quickly to besiege the Castle of Ager, defended by Neapolitan Tercio of Pietro de Orellana. On 6th October

the French were in front of the castle with their two guns in action. In less than four days the Italian garrison surrendered and Condé installed Catalan troops to occupy Ager. During the siege the army of Aytona remained static around Lleida, the Spanish general had strict orders not to risk a battle against Condé. On 10th October, Aytona sent an order to Francisco Tuttavilla to attack the French position of Constanti with tercios from the garrison of Tarragona and a tercio from the armada. On 24th October, Tuttavilla, with the support of six guns, created a breach in the wall of the castle of Constanti and immediately launched an assault. The Spanish were repulsed by the garrison and, on the news that French reinforcements under the command of Marshal Gramont were arriving, Tuttavilla fell back to Tarragona as quick as possible. Thanks to the quick reaction of Condé, the operation ended in failure. Gramont stayed some days to repair the walls and to boost the garrison. Meantime, the Marques of Aytona wanted to attack either the diminished force of Condé, or that of Gramont, and moved to les Borques Blanques. The coordinated movement of Gramont and Condé prevented this action and this time Aytona had to withdraw rapidly to Lleida and Fraga, while the opposing cavalry skirmished with each other. Exhausted after a long campaign and with no will to fight a pitch battle, Aytona decided to send all his troops into winter quarters. On the French side, the Prince of Condé was eager to obtain the latest news from Paris where the young king had caught smallpox, at that time a terrible disease for a 9 years old boy. For Condé, his future was in Paris and he had nothing to do in Catalonia, so in November 1647 he went back to France.

---

two Irish Tercios of Preston and Fitzgerald, and the German Regiment of Grosfeit.

[67] In June 1646, the Marques of Aytona gathered in Fraga a force of 11,000 Foot (26 tercios/regiments), divided in 4,200 veterans (Spanish, Italians, Walloons, Irish and Germans) from previous campaigns, 2,300 new recruits (mostly Spanish), 2,300 men from the garrison of Tarragona and Tortosa and 2,000 men from Aragon.

Chapter 4
Epilogue ~ The Road to Barcelona

At the beginning of 1648, the city of Lleida was still a vanguard for the Spanish position in Catalonia, and Balaguer, Flix, Cervera and Ager were still controlled by Franco-Catalan forces. The Spanish monarchy was bogged by multiple rebellions, particularly by the revolt in Naples[1] and could not dedicate the required human and financial resources to take the offensive in Catalonia.

In fact in Catalonia, contrary to expectations, it was the French who were on the offensive. In May, Charles of Schonberg, Duke of Haluin, was nominated viceroy of Catalonia to replace Michel of Mazarin, Cardinal of Sainte Cécile. In June he mustered 10,000 men[2] south of Barcelona and decided to attack the city of Tortosa, defended by Diego de Brizuela with a garrison of 1,000–1,500 regular soldiers and 1,000 militia and armed civilians from the city. On 10th June a French vanguard arrived near Tortosa. With the arrival of more troops, they managed to cross the river Ebro and took the town of Ulldecona 25 km south of Tortosa. With the support of the fleet, the French also controlled the mouth of the river, and used it to transport the heavy artillery guns for the siege. On the Spanish side the

new commander, Francisco de Melo,[3] attempted a diversion and on 19th June he appeared in front of Flix. With a quick movement, the French general managed to introduce reinforce-ments and established himself near the city with 6,000–7,000 men, while the remaining third were in front of Tortosa. Francisco de Melo had received orders to avoid battle and so refused to confront the French, after a short demon-stration he returned to Lleida and Fraga. The French returned to the siege and the operation continued, it was expected that Tortosa could hold out until the end of July. Unfortunately for the Spanish, French soldiers managed to enter the city through a small breach on 12th July. To avoid further loss of life, the capitulation of the city was concluded the next day. The same day, the explosion of a store full of black powder killed 200 French-men and lead to a savage sacking of the city where no building was saved from the rapacity of the French troops.

The victory was of little use to the Catalans because the situation in Paris was changing. Mazarin had dedicated too much effort, money and men with few successes in Catalonia. In fact the situation in France was not as good as it seemed. To finance the participation of the French monarchy in the Thirty Years War, Richelieu, and later Mazarin, had increased taxes significantly. By the spring of 1648 the fiscal pressure was so great that there was general discontent among all classes of the population. On 15th June this discontent exploded during a session of the parliament of Paris. For some

---

[1] Until now Naples had been one of the major providers, along with Castilla, of money and troops for the monarchy, but that was no longer possible. The revolt of Naples from 1647 to 1651 against Spanish authority was the consequence of the constraints induced by decades of wars and the rash actions of some of the Spanish viceroys.

[2] In fact the army was commanded by Ferdinand de Marchin and had – Infantry, 7,000 men: 10 French regiments, 2 Swiss regiments and 2 Catalan regiments; Cavalry, 3,000 men: 6 companies of Guards, Gend-armes and Chevaux-Légers, 11 French regiments, 1 German regiment and 2 Catalan regiments.

[3] Francisco de Melo has been Governor of Flanders from 1641 to 1644. He is best remembered for being the general who lost the battle of Rocroi on 19th May 1643.

months Mazarin attempted negotiations, but the victory of Lens offered an opportunity, at the end of August, to re-establish civil order by force – a civil war (1648–1652) commenced in France, known as *la Fronde*. For Catalonia the outbreak of the Fronde meant that France would reduce funds and adopt a defensive position in its territory.

In 1649, both the Spanish and French monarchies were involved in the suppression of multiple revolts against the financial and human burdens required to sustain the war. In Catalonia, a new Spanish commander, Juan de Garay, was appointed. With a reduced, but select, army he conducted a campaign around Tarragona and the south of Barcelona, taking several small fortified cities, such as Montblanc, Salou, Constanti and Sitges. On the French side, the strong garrison of Tortosa launched raids to lay waste the north of the province of Valencia which up to that point had been spared the atrocities of war.[4]

The next year, the new French viceroy, the Duke of Mercoeur, tried to retake the Castle of Castèll-Lleó in the Val d'Aran valley in the Pyrenees. On 1st May he entered the valley with a force of 3,000 men and two half-canons. Receiving this news, the Spanish quickly organized a force of 1,700–1,800 men[5] under the command of Francisco Tuttavilla. On 25th May the Spanish managed to dislodge the French from their positions and to force them into an inglorious retreat. At the same time, in Tuscany, the Spanish had retaken the castles of Piombino and Portolongone, while order was restored in

most of the kingdom of Naples. These successes gave them the opportunity to redeploy troops engaged in southern Italy to Catalonia, and to the Army of Lombardia. In Catalonia the Marques of Mortara had replaced Juan de Garay and, at the beginning of September, launched a full-scale operation to recover the control of the river Ebro. With an army of some 9,000 men, he managed to mislead the French command and besiege Flix, defended by only 300 men. The Duke of Mercoeur, with a Franco-Catalan army of 4,000 Foot and 2,500 Horse, crossed the river Ebro and went to Ascò, a few kilometres from the Spanish positions. Unfortunately for the French general, all his efforts to reinforce the garrison ended in failure and on 25th September the governor of Flix, Monsieur de Sainte Colonne, capitulated. The next target was the Castle of Miravet, defended by 200 Frenchmen. After two weeks of siege, including a week of bombardment, the castle capitulated on 15th October. Mortora took his time to reorganize his army and to coordinate, with the Spanish fleet, his next action – against Tortosa. By the middle of November, the Spanish were in front of Tortosa, which was defended by a strong garrison. The Franco-Catalan field army was not strong enough to challenge the Spanish army and on 24th November a French squadron of four ships with supplies and reinforcements was destroyed off the Catalan coast; the blockade of Tortosa was complete. Ten days later, the French governor of Tortosa capitulated. With the conquest of Flix, Mirabet, and the recovery of Tortosa, the road to Barcelona was now open.

In 1651, with the arrival of Juan de Austria as commander in chief of the Army of Catalonia and with reinforce-ments from Italy, the operation against the capital of Catalonia could finally start. In July 1651, the Marques of Mortara set out from Lleida in direction of Tarragona with an army of 6,000 Foot, 3,000 Horse and 16 artillery pieces. In Tarragona he was joined by Juan de Austria, with the Spanish fleet, 2,500 Foot and more artillery. By the end of August an army of

---

[4] The province of Valencia was preserved from the war but not from the plague. Since 1647, the province had been swept by an epidemic of plague responsible for killing 16,000 people. For the Catalans, one of the most terrible consequences of the raids was that soldiers returned with contaminated clothing to Tortosa. The plague broke out in the city and spread along the Catalan coast, especially in the regions of Barcelona and Girona.

[5] Following Parets [*Memorial Historico* Vol. 24], the composition of the Spanish army was 1,100 Foot, extracted from three Spanish tercios (Tercio of la Guardia, the Tercio of Pedro Estevan and the Tercio of Francisco Sada), the German Regiment of Seebach, 400 light infantry from Aragon and Val d'Aran, and 250 Horse.

only 11,000 men[6] was advancing, without opposition, toward Barcelona, defended by some 10,000 men (7,000 regulars and 3,000 militia). With so few men, only a strategic blockade could be undertaken by the Spanish. Over the next 15 months fierce fighting would occur whenever the French and Catalans tried to breach the Spanish stranglehold. Most of these efforts would end in failure and the Spanish always managed to restore their position. At last, on 11th October 1652, with no hope of relief, Barcelona capitulated.

In Catalonia, the Thirty Years War was not over, but for the next six years, fighting and military operations would take place around the actual border between France and Spain.

[6] An estimation of the Spanish strength around Barcelona in 1651 gives: 8,500 Foot in 10 Spanish tercios (Tercio of la Cueva, Tercio del Castillo, Tercio of Torres, Tercio of Cavallero, Tercio of Viedna, Tercio of Tarragona, Tercio of Estevan, Tercio of Sada, Tercio of Azlor and Tercio of Valencia), 4 Italian tercios (Tercio of Garaffa, Tercio of Genaro, Tercio of Rho and Tercio of Grez), 3 Walloon tercios (Tercio of Calonne, Tercio of Clerc and Tercio of Franque), 2 Irish tercios (Tercio of O'Brien and Tercio of Tyrone) and 5 German regiments (Regiment of Laques, Regiment of Kleinhans, Regiment of Vilani, Regiment of Carene and Regiment of Chapuis); 2,500 Horse,

References

Pre 1930

Aumale, Henri d'Orléans; *Histoire des princes de Condé pendant les siècles XVI et XVII par le Duc d'Aumale.* Vol. 5. Paris 1889.

Barado, Francisco; *Museo Militar, Historia del ejército español ….. Tomo 3*, Barcelona 1887.

Catalán, Jimenéz. *Don Gregorio de Brito.* Revista de archivos, bibliotecas y museos tomo 38 & 39. Madrid 1919.

Clonard, Conde de; *Historia orgánica de las armas de infantería y caballería españolas desde la creación del ejército permanente hasta el día.* Vol. 4 and 9. Madrid 1851.

Colección de Documentos Inéditos para la Historia de España (CODOIN), edited by the Marques de la Fuensanta de Valls. Tome 87, 95 and 97 contains documents relating to the War of the Reapers 1641–1649. Madrid 1895.

Corresponding letters of fathers from the Companies of Jesus covering events of the years 1640 to 1648. *Memorial Histórico Español: Colección de Documentos Opúsculos y Antigüedades*, Vol. 16, 17, 18 and 19. Published by the Spanish Royal Academy in Madrid, 1864-1865.

Feliu de la Peña y Farell, Narcis; *Anales de Cataluña y epilogo breve de los progressos, y famosos hechos de la nación catalana... hasta el presente de 1709*, Vol. 3. Barcelona 1709.

Gaya, Louis de. *Traité des armes, des machines de guerre… et des Instruments Militaires.* Paris 1678.

Gramont, Antoine de. *Mémoires du maréchal de Gramont. Collection des Mémoire relative à l'Histoire de France*, Edition Petitot, Paris 1826.

Informe del duque de Cardona sobre la empresa de Loecata Carpeta: Perpiñàn.-A S. Md. (A su Majestad), 1637; Archivo General de Simancas, *Registro Guerra Antigua, 1186.*

Mazarin, Jules (1602-1661). *Lettres du cardinal Mazarin pendant son ministère.* Tome II. Publié par M. A. Cheruel, Collection de Documents Inéduts sur l'Hitoire de France. Paris 1879.

Mello, Francisco *Manuel de. historia de los movimientos, separación y guerra de Cataluña en tiempo de Felipe IV.* Universidad de Cadiz 1842.

Mémoires de François de Paule de Clermont, marquis de Montglat, *Contenant l'Histoire de la guerre entre la France et la maison d'Autriche ……* in *Nouvelle collection des mémoires pour servir à l'histoire de France depuis le XIIIe siècle jusqu'à la fin du XVIIIe siècle*, Michaud, J-F / Poujoulat J.-J.-F. (Éd).

Novoa, Matías de. *Memorias de un ayudante de cámara de Felipe IV.* Colección de Documentos Inéditos para la Historia de España (CODOIN) Vol. 86, edited by the Marques de la Fuensanta de Valls. Madrid 1895.

Paret, Miguel; *Crónica de Cataluña 1640-1660. Memorial Histórico Español: Colección de Documentos Opúsculos y Antigüedades*, Vol. 20 to 25. Published by the Spanish Royal Academy in Madrid, 1864-1865.

Pinard. *Chronologie historique-militaire, contenant l'histoire de la création de toutes les charges, dignités et grades militaires supérieurs, de toutes les personnes qui les ont possédés… …………* Tome 1, 2, 4 & 6 Paris 1760-1778.

Plessis-Besançons; *Mémoires de Du Plessis-Besançon*, publiés pour la Société de l'histoire de France et accompagnés de correspondances et de documents inédits. Paris 1892.

Salas y Cortes, Ramon de; *Memorial Histórico de la Artillería Española.* Madrid 1831.

Ufano, Diego de. *Artillerie, c'est à dire Vraye instruction de l'artillerie et de toutes ses appartenances.* Zutphen 1621.

Valladares de Sotomayor, Antonio; *Semanario erudito que comprehende varias obras ineditas*, criticas ..... Vol. 31, 32 and 33. Madrid 1890.

Most of the references can be found in pdf form, from the portals of National libraries such as the *Biblioteca national de España* (http://www.bne.es), the *Bibliothèques national de France* (http://www.gallica.fr), the British Library (http://www.bl.uk/) or in the Internet Archive (http://archive.org/).

Post 1930

J.L. Ancón & L.P. Martínez (1998). *En torno al mural del moli dels frares: los asedios de Salses en 1639*. Reseaching & Dragona nº5, p104.

J. Burgueño (2001). *Atles de les viles, ciutats i territoris de Lleida*. Diputació de Lleida : Col·legi d'Arquitectes de Catalunya. Demarcació de Lleida, 2001, 603 pages; ISBN 8488258879.

J. H. Elliott (1963). *The Revolt of the Catalans: a study in the decline of Spain (1598-1640)*. Cambridge University Press, 623 pages; ISBN 0521278902.

G. Foard (2009). *Guidance on Recording Lead Bullets from Early Modern Battlefields*, *www.heritagescience.ac.uk/*.

J.L. Gonzales, A. Riber & O. Uceda (1999). *El Setges de Lleida 1644-1647*. Edition ILTRA, 154 pages; ISBN 8489781117.

M. Güell, Manuel (2006). *Expugnare Oppidum: el setge de Condé (Lleida, 1647)*. A Carn! nº 2, http://blocs.tinet.cat/acarn/numeros/

F.-X. Hernández, *Història Militar de Catalunya, Vol. III: La defensa de la Terra*, RAFAEL DALMAU, Editor, 2003, 340 pages; ISBN 9788423206643

Ignacio J.N. López (2012). *The Spanish Tercios 1536–1704*. Osprey, Men-at-Arms 481, 48 pages; ISBN 9781849087933.

D. Maffi (2008). *Il Valuardo della Corona. Guerre Esercito, Finanze e Societa' Nella Lombarda Seicentesa (1630-1660)*. Edition LE MONNIER, 472 pages; ISBN 9788800206600.

E. Martinez-Ruis (2008). *Los Soldados del Rey: Los ejércitos de la Monarquía Hispánica (1480-1700)*. Edition CORONA BOREALIS, 1070 pages; ISBN 9788497390736.

J. H. Muñoz-Sebastià & E. Querol-Coll (2004). *La Guerra dels Segadors a Tortosa (1640-1651)*. Edition COSSETANIA. 345 pages; ISBN 8497910699.

A. Passola-Tejedor (2004). *Historia de lleida* Volum 5. Edition PAGES, 355 pages; ISBN 5 :8497791290.

P. Picouet (2010). *Les Tercios espagnols: 1600-1660*. Edition LRT, 140 pages; ISBN 9782917747056.

L. Ribot Garcia (1983). *El ejercito de los Austrias. Aportaciones recientes y nuevas perpctivas*. Temas de Historia Militar, t. I, Madrid.

L. Ribot Garcia (1990). *Milan Plaza de armas de la monarquia. Investigaciones históricas: Época moderna y contemporánea*, ISSN 0210-9425, Nº 10, págs. 203-238

P. Sanz-Camañes (2001). *Un Conflicto de jurisdicciones*. "Alojamiento y guerra de frontera" RHM nº22.

S. Thion (2008). *French Armies of the Thirty Years War*. Edition LRT. 172 pages. ISBN 9782947747018.

L. White (2003). *Guerra y Revolución Militar en la Iberia del Siglo XVII*, Manuscrits 21, 62-93.

E. Zudaire-Huarte (1960). *Empresa de Leucata, lance fatal del virrey Cardona, 29 de agosto-29 de septiembre de 1637* Institut d'Estudis Gironins (Annals) Vol. 14; Pàgina: 85-116.

Internet

www.tercio.org : website by Juan Luis Sanchez-Martin

guerrasegadors.blogspot.com.es : blogs from Àlex Claramunt Soto

guerradarestauracao.wordpress.com

tercio1617.net46.net/home.html : website by Pierre A. Picouet

Tables and Annexes

Table 1a: Main Officers of the Spanish Army of Catalonia during 1643- 1648

Year	General Captain	Maestro de Campo General	General Captain of the Cavalry	General Captain of the Artillery
1643	Felipe da Silva	Juan de Garay	Marques of Mortara	Francisco de Tuttavilla
1644	Felipe da Silva Andrea Cantelmo	Juan de Garay Marques of Mortara	Juan de Vivaro	Francisco de Tuttavilla
1645	Andrea Cantelmo Felipe da Silva	Marques of Mortara	Duke of Alburquerque.	N.D.
1646	Marques of Leganés	Baron of Seebach Francisco de Tuttavilla	Duke of Infantado	Tiberio Brancaccio
1647	Marques of Aytona	Marques of Mortara	Duke of Alburquerque	Tiberio Brancaccio
1648	Francisco de Melo	Marques of Mortara	Duke of Alburquerque	Francisco de Tejada

Table 1b: Main Officers of the French Army of Catalonia during 1643- 1647

Year	Viceroy	Marshal of France	Lieutnants Generals	Field Marshals (1)
1643	Philippe de la Mothe-Houdancourt	Philippe de la Mothe-Houdancourt	N.D.	Lord of Ferracières; Baron du Terrail, Marquis of Vandy; Count of Tournon; Count of Chabot
1644	Philippe de la Mothe-Houdancourt	Philippe de la Mothe-Houdancourt	Count of Du Plessis	Lord of Ferracières; Baron du Terrail; Olivier de Castellan; Marquis of Vandy; Count of Chabot
1645	Henri de Lorraine Count of Harcourt	Henri de Lorraine Count of Harcourt	Count of Du Plessis-Pralins	Baron du Terrail; Count of Chabot; Marquis of Saint Aunets; Marquis of La Trousse; Bernard du Plessis-Besançon
1646	Henri de Lorraine Count of Harcourt	Henri de Lorraine Count of Harcourt	Count of Couvonges	Count of Chabot; Marquis of Gesvres; Count of Illes (2); Marquis of La Trousse; Marquis de Montpezat; Marquis of Marins; André de Boissac; Knight of La Vallière; François de Maugiron
1647	Prince of Condé	Duke of Gramont	Count of de Manicamp Count of Marchins	Marquis of La Moussaye; Marquis of Saint Aunets; Marquis of La Trousse; Marquis de Montpezat; Marquis of Marins; André de Boissac, Knight of La Vallière; Marquis de Persan; Charles Le Ferron

(1) The table is probably incomplete.
(2) Josep d'Ardennes d'Aragó, Count of Illes, was a Catalan officer.

Table 2a: Estimation of the effective strength of the Spanish army in Catalonia and Aragon between 1643 and 1647

	Field Army			Garrison
	Infantry	Cavalry	Total	(estimated)
October 1643 [1]	8,500 men	3,900 men [2]	12,400 men	≈ 11,000 men
April 1644 [3]	9,554 men	4,336 men [3]	13,892 men	≈ 10,000 men
September 1644	> 9,000 men	2,600 men	12,000 men	-
June 1645 [4]	8,000 men	3,000 men	11,000 men	≈ 13,000 men
October 1646 [5]	> 12,000 men	3,500 men	15,500 men	≈ 11,000 men
June 1647 [6]	10,000 men	3,200 men	13,000 men	< 9,000 men
October 1647 [7]	8,000 men	2,000 men	11,000 men	>12,000 men

1. Aviso del 3 de Noviembre 1643, Semanario erudito Tomo 33. V. Balaguer [*Historia de Catalunya* tomo 8] gives 13,000 men divided between 10,000 Foot and 3,000 Horse
2. The number given is for 3,600 cavalry and 300 dragoons
3. Review of 29th April 1644, Campaña de 1644, CODOIN vol. 95. For the cavalry, the total is 3,734 mounted and 602 dismounted.
4. Novoa, CODOIN Vol. 86.
5. Number given by J.L. Gonzales et al. (1999).
6. Estimation, extracted from Catalán (1919)
7. Aumale, *Histoire des Princes de Condé* vol 5.

Table 2b: Estimation of the effective strength of the French field army in Catalonia between 1643 and 1647

	Field Army		
	Infantry	Cavalry	Total
November 1643	8,500 men	2,500 men	11,000 men
May 1644 [1]	> 7,000 men	1,800 men	> 9,000 men
August 1644	8,500 men	2,500 men	12,000 men
June 1645	10,000 men	2,500 men	12,500 men
April 1646 [2]	12,000 men	5,500 men	17,500 men
April 1647 [3]	10,000 men	4,000 men	14,000 men

1. Excluding the garrison of Lleida
2. Pradet [*Memorial Historico* Vol. 24]
3. Aumale, *Histoire des Princes de Condé* vol 5.

Table 3: French Army of 27th May 1647, following a Spanish document [CODOIN 95]. The names of French regiments have been updated using the information from Susane (*Histoire de l'Infanterie et de la cavalerie française*). Unfortunately some regiments remain difficult to trace, especially that of Beins and Pomenare.

	Infantry	Cavalry
Quarter of Villanoveta (South)	Rgt. of Guyenne (French) Rgt. of Amboise (French) Rgt. of Jerbes (French) Rgt. of Rhoom (French)	Rgt. of Count of Marchins
Quarter of the King (North-east)	Rgt. of Champagne (French) Rgt. of Praroman (Swiss) (1)	Company of Guards of Condé Company of Gendarmes of Condé French Volunteers Rgt. of Condé-Cavalerie Rgt. of Mazarin-Italien (2) Rgt. of Angluer (Aguilar-Catalan?)
Quarter of Balthazard (west on the road to Aragón)	Rgt. of Nerestang (French) Rgt. of Condé-Infanterie (French) Rgt. of the Prince of Conti (French)	Rgt. of the Count of Balthazard
Quarter of Pont de Gaut	Rgt. of Périgord (French)	Rgt. of Pont de Gaut-Italien
Quarter of Beins	Rgt. of Enghien (French) Rgt. of Rham (Swiss)	Rgt. of Beins Rgt. of the Duke of Créqui
Quarter of Gramont	Rgt. of Persan (French) Rgt. of Lorraine (French)	Company of Guards of Gramont Company of Chevau-Légers of Condé Rgt. of the Baron of Alais Rgt. of Pomenar Rgt. of Calvo Rgt. of de la Mothe-Houdancourt

(1) It could also be the Regiment of Rham.
(2) In 1647 Cardinal Mazarin had three regiments of cavalry (Mazarin-Français, Mazarin-Etranger and Mazarin-Italien).

Annex I: Main tercios and regiments of the Spanish infantry present in Catalonia between 1643 and 1647. The table is based on sources cited in the Bibliography and the website of J.L. Sanchez (www.tercios.org). Two triangles (▶▶) indicated that the unit participated in one of the major action of that year and one triangle (▶) indicated that the unit was probably operational in this year.

Spanish / Regular	Main Commaders	1643	1644	1645	1646	1647
Regiment de la Guardia del Rey ("Viejo")	*1643 Josef Calderon* *1643 Simón de Mascareña* *1646 Pablo Paradas* *1647 Pedro Valenzuela* *1650 Pedro Orteriz*	▶▶	▶▶	▶▶	▶▶	▶▶
Tercio "Viejo" de Lisboa	*1641: Diego de Aguilera* *1650: Cristóbal Caballero*	▶▶	▶▶	▶▶	▶▶	▶▶
Regiment of the Principe ("Viejo") (1)	*1642 Enrique de Guzmán* *1644 Pardo de la Casta* *1645 No Information*	▶▶	▶▶	▶▶	▶	
Tercio "Viejo" de Villamayor	*Alonso de Villamayor*			▶	▶▶	▶
Tercio "Viejo" de Villalba	*Diego de Villalba*		▶	▶	▶▶	
Tercio de Vagos	*Luis de Silva*			▶	▶▶	▶
Tercio de los Arcos	*Simón de Mascareña*	▶▶				
Tercio de Parada	*Pablo de Parada*	▶▶	▶▶			
Tercio de Mújica	*Martin de Mújica*	▶▶	▶▶			
Tercio de Ascárraga	*Esteban de Ascárraga*	▶	▶▶	▶		
Tercio de Freire	*Francisco Freire*	▶	▶▶	▶		
Tercio de Osteriz	*Pedro Osteriz*			▶▶	▶▶	▶▶
Tercio de Valenzuela	*Pedro Valenzuela*			▶▶		
Tercio de Quiñones	*Diego de Quiñones*			▶	▶▶	▶
Regiment of Aguilar	*Conde of Aguilar*				▶	▶▶
Regiment t of Hinojosa	*Fernando de Galindo*	▶▶				
Tercio de Garcés	*Juan de Garcés Mendoza*				▶▶	▶
Tercio "Viejo" de Napoles	*Cristóbal Salgado*				▶▶	▶
Tercio de Priego	*Marqués de Priego*				▶	▶
Tercio de Soriano	*Clémente de Soriano*	▶▶	▶▶			
Spanish / Armada (2)						
Tercio of Velasco	*Francisco de Velasco*	▶▶				
Tercio of Benavides	*Juan de Benavides*			▶	▶▶	▶
Tercio of Sotomayor	*Luis de Sotomayor*		▶	▶▶	▶▶	▶
Tercio of Galeones	*Rodrigo Niño de Mendoza*				▶▶	▶▶
Tercio of Ledesna	*Francisco de Ledesna*				▶	
Spanish / Provincial						
Tercio "Viejo" de Navarra	*1642 Jerónimo de Ayanz* *1644 Baltazar de Rada* *1646 Josef Beaumonte*	▶	▶▶	▶▶	▶▶	▶
Tercio of León	*Marques de Lorenzana*				▶▶	▶▶
Tercio of Andalucía	*Don Pedro de Angulo*	▶	▶▶			
Tercio of Castillas	*Condestable of Castillas*		▶▶			
Tercio of Luna	*Count of Luna*		▶▶			
Tercio(s) of Valencia (3)	*Jeronomi Mansiari*		▶▶		▶▶	▶▶
Tercio Viejo of Zaragoza	*1642 : Francisco de Funes* *1646: Don Diego de Francia*		▶▶	▶	▶▶	▶
Tercio of Letosa (Aragon)	*Barón de Letosa*		▶▶			
Tercio of Marco (Aragon)	*Marco Antonio Março*			▶	▶▶	▶
Tercio of Templado (Aragon)	*Don Joseph Templado*			▶	▶▶	▶
Nation / Walloons	Main Commaders					
Tercio of Van der Straeten (4)	*André Van der Straeten*	▶	▶▶	▶	▶▶	▶
Tercio de Calonne	*1639, Marquis of Molinghen* *1644 Charles A. de Calonne*	▶	▶▶	▶	▶▶	▶
Tercio of Mande	*Pierre de Mande*		▶▶			
Tercio of Gronsfelt	*Count of Gronsfelt*		▶▶	▶▶	▶	

Nation / Italians						
Tercio de Amato	*Baron of Amato*	▶	▶▶	▶▶	▶▶	▶▶
Tercio of Brancaccio	*Frey Pietro de Brancaccio*	▶▶	▶▶	▶▶	▶▶	▶
Tercio of Cerdeña	*Marques of Villasor*	▶▶				
Tercio of Laurenzana	*Duque of Laurenzana*	▶	▶▶	▶▶		
Tercio of Mata	*Baron of Mata*			▶▶		
Tercio of Poticque	*No Information*			▶▶		
Tercio de Pignatiello	*Scipio Pignatiello*				▶▶	
Tercio de San Felices [5]	*Fabio de San felice*				▶▶	
Tercio de Orellana	*Pietro de Orellana*				▶▶	▶▶
Mercenaries / Germans						
Regiment of Galaso	*No Information*	▶	▶▶			
Regiment of Grosfeit	*No Information*				▶▶	▶▶
Regiment of Seebach	*Baron of Seebach*		▶▶	▶▶	▶▶	▶
Regiment of Hamel	*Ludwig von Hamel*			▶▶	▶	▶▶
Mercenaries / Irish						
Tercio of Preston	*James Preston*		▶	▶▶	▶▶	
Tercio of O'Brien	*Christopher O'Brien*	▶	▶▶	▶	▶	▶
Tercio of Fitzgerald	*Patrick Fitzgerald*		▶▶	▶	▶▶	

(1) Following Count of Clonard, the regiment was formed in March 1642 and disbanded in November 1646 after the death of the Principe, Baltasar Carlos, on 20th August 1645.

(2) Even if the tercio have been recruited in Naples, it was part of the galley squadron of Naples and therefore part of the Spanish Armada.

(3) Valencia regularly sent *tropos*/tercios to reinforce the garrisons of Tortosa and Tarragona, but in 1644 they send the Tercio of Mansiari to be incorporated into the Army of Catalonia at Fraga.

(4) The tercio arrived in 1638 in Spain under the command of Balthazar Philippe of Gand, Count of Isenghien

(5) Even if the tercio have been recruited in Naples, it was part of the galley squadron of Naples and therefore part of the Spanish Armada.

Annex II: Main regiments of the French infantry presents in Catalonia between 1643 and 1647. This table is based on sources cited in the Bibliography. Two triangles (▶▶) indicated that the unit participated in one of the major action of that year and one triangle (▶) indicated that the unit was probably operational in this year.

White Flag French regiments	Commanders	1643	1644	1645	1646	1647
Gardes Suisses	*4 companies*			▶▶(1)		
Normandie	*Count of Frontenac*			▶▶(1)		
Champagne	*1635 Count of Origny (KIA 1646)* *1648 Count of Broglio*			▶▶	▶▶	▶▶
Sault	*Count of Sault*			▶▶(1)		
Nérestang / Saint Mesme	*1639 Marquis of Nérestang* *1645 Count of Saint-Mesme*		▶▶	▶▶	▶▶	▶▶
Lyonnais	*Lord of Alincourt*	▶▶	▶▶	▶▶(1)		
French Regiments						
Vaubécourt / Entragues	*1628 Count of Vaubécourt* *1646 Count of Entragues*			▶▶	▶▶	
Lorraine	*Count of Couvonges (KIA 1646)*				▶▶	
Vaillac	*Count of Vaillac*		▶▶	▶	▶▶	▶▶
Tournon (2)	*Count of Tournon-Roussillon*	▶	▶▶			
Ferrières	*Baron of Ferrières*			▶▶	▶▶	
Saint–Paul	*Balthazard of Saint –Paul*		▶▶	▶▶(1)		
Ventadour	*Duke of Ventadour*		▶▶	▶▶		
Mirepoix	*Baron of Mirepoix*	▶▶	▶	▶▶	▶▶	▶▶
Tonneins / Monpouillan	*164x Marquis of Tonneins* *1644 Marquis of Monpouillan*	▶▶	▶▶	▶▶	▶▶	▶▶
Saint Aunetz	*Marquis of Saint Aunetz*					▶▶
Vervin	*Marquis of Vervin*		▶▶			
Tavannes	*Marquis of Tavannes*		▶▶	▶▶(1)		
Le Ferron	*Charles Claude Le Ferron*		▶▶	▶▶	▶▶	▶▶
Roquelaure	*Marquis of Roquelaure*	▶▶	▶▶			
de la Mothe-Houdancourt	*Philippe de la Mothe-Houdancourt*	▶▶	▶▶	▶▶	▶▶	
Marchin	*Count of Marchin*					▶▶
Vandy	*Marquis of Vandy*	▶▶	▶▶			
Rébé	*Baron of Rébé*	▶▶	▶▶	▶▶(1)	▶▶	▶▶
Huxelles	*Marquis of Huxelles*		▶▶	▶▶(1)		
Montpezat	*Marquis of Montpezat*			▶▶	▶▶	
Enghien	*Duke of Enghien*					▶▶
Perigord	*Marquis of Rasilly*				▶▶	▶▶
La Marine	*Marquis of La Trousse*	▶▶		▶▶	▶▶	▶▶
Conti	*Prince of Conti*					▶▶
Boissy	*Marquis of Boissy*		▶			
Poitou	*Chastellier Barot*	▶	▶▶	▶▶(1)		
Saintonge	*Marquis of Albret*		▶▶	▶▶	▶▶	▶▶
Guyenne	*Duke of Eperon*			▶▶	▶▶	▶▶
Harcourt	*Count of Harcourt*			▶▶	▶▶	▶▶
Calvisson	*1642 Lord of Calvisson*		▶▶			
Montpeyroux	*Vicomte de Montpeyroux*	▶▶	▶	▶▶	▶▶	▶▶
Gesvres	*1642 Marquis de Gesvres (KIA 1646)* *1647 Duke of Gesvres*			▶▶	▶▶	
Fabert	*Abraham Fabert*				▶▶	
Caderousse	*Lord of Caderousse*			▶▶(1)		
Palliers	*Lord of Palliers*			▶▶		
Beaufort	*Duc de Beaufort*			▶▶(1)		
Anduze	*Lord of Anduze*			▶▶(1)		
Ruvigny	*Marquis of Ruvigny*		▶▶			
Condé-Infanterie	*Prince of Condé*					▶▶
Mérinville-Infanterie	*Marquis Mérinville*			▶▶	▶▶	▶▶
Calvière	*Lord of Calvière*			▶▶(1)		
la Vallière	*Chevalier de la Vallière*					▶▶
Swiss Regiment						
Rhan	*Jean Jacque Rahn*		▶			
Praromann	*Jacques Nicolas Praromann*			▶		

Am Büchel	*Balthazar Am Büchel*	►►			
Rhoom	*Coronel Rhoom*		►►	►►	►►
Catalan Regiment					
Aguilar	*Josep of Marguerit, Marquis of Aguilar*				►►
Sénister	*Lord Sénister*				►►
Ardenne	*Josep d'Ardenne d'Aragó*				►►

(1) These regiments only participated in the siege of Rosas in spring 1645; later on most of them were transferred to Toulon to participate in the campaign of Orbetello in 1646.
(2) In some French sources the regiment is called Roussillon.

The Pike and Shot Society
Warfare in the Early Modern World 1400 - 1720

We hope you have enjoyed reading this publication and that, if you are not already a member of the *Pike and Shot Society*, you may wish to consider joining.

Founded in 1973, the *Pike and Shot Society* is an international society that promotes interest in the warfare of the early-modern period, a time that saw radical change in the way in which wars were fought world-wide. Its main activity is the publication of its highly respected bi-monthly journal *Arquebusier* as well as specialist books, monographs and booklets such as this.

Arquebusier reflects the interests and researches of its members and other military historians. Authors offer material free of charge so the Society keeps its subscription to the minimum. The international nature of the Society means that it has access to unique material, which it publishes for the benefit of members.

In addition to *Arquebusier*, Society members benefit from discounts on a wide range of books and other products of interest. Although based in Great Britain, it is an important aim of the Society to recruit members from around the world. Details of the Society and membership information can be found on our website at:

<u>www.pikeandshotsociety.org</u>

or by writing to:

The Pike and Shot Society,
℅ 16 Cobbetts Way
Farnham
Surrey
GU9 8TL
Great Britain

Publications of the Pike and Shot Society

Uniforms and Colours of the Wars of Louis XIV

- *Flags and Uniforms of the French Infantry under Louis XIV, 1688-1714* by Robert Hall
- *Standards and Uniforms of the French Cavalry under Louis XIV, 1688-1714* by Robert Hall, Giancarlo Boeri & Yves Roumegoux
- *Guidons, Flags and Uniforms of the French Dragoons, Militia, Artillery and Bombardiers under Louis XIV, 1688-1714* by Robert Hall, Yves Roumegoux & Giancarlo Boeri
- *The Army of the Electorate Palatine under Elector Johann Wilhelm 1690-1716* by Claus-Peter Golberg & Robert Hall
- *The Armies of Hesse and the Upper Rhine Circle* by Robert Hall
- *Uniforms and Flags of the Imperial Austrian Army 1683–1720* by Robert Hall and Giancarlo Boeri
- *Spanish Armies in the War of the League of Augsburg, 1688–1697* by Giancarlo Boeri, Josè Luis Mirecki and Josè Palau
- *The Army of the Duke of Savoy 1688 – 1713* by Giancarlo Boeri, with the collaboration of Roberto Vela, Giovanni Cerino Badone and Robert Hall

Renaissance Military Texts Series

- Vol. 1: *Warfare in the Age of Louis XIV.* Three contemporary military tracts from the late 17th and early 18th centuries. Edited by Neil Rennoldson

Other Society Books

- *'An ill jurney for the Englishemen': Elis Gruffydd and the 1523 French Campaign of the Duke of Suffolk.* Transcribed by M. Bryn Davies and edited with a new introduction by Jonathan Davies
- *Elis Gruffydd and the 1544 'Enterprises' of Paris and Boulogne.* Transcribed by M. Bryn Davies and edited with a new introduction by Jonathan Davies.
- *Thomas Audley and the Tudor Art of War* by Jonathan Davies
- *The English Companies of Foot in 1588* by Jonathan Davies
- *The Struggle for Stralsund 1627-1630* by Don McNair
- *La Scherma (The Art of Fencing, 1640)* by Francesco Ferdinando Alfieri. Translated and edited by Caroline Stewart, Phil Marshall & Piermarco Terminiello
- *Waller's Army. The Regiments of Sir William Waller's Southern Association* by L. Spring
- *Lostwithiel 1644–The Campaign and Battles* by Stephen Ede-Borrett
- *'Uncharitable Mischief': Barbarity and Excess in the British Civil Wars* by Charles Singleton
- *The Art of Gunnery (1647) together with A Treatise of Artificall Fire-Works (1647) by Nathanael Nye.* Introduction and Transcription by Cliff Mitchell
- *Enniskillen and the Battle of Newtownbutler, 1689* by D.P. Graham
- *Brothers in Arms: The Hamiltons in Ireland, England and France 1610-1719* by D.P. Graham
- *Marlborough Goes to War* by Iain Stanford
- *Eight Banners and Green Flag. The Army of the Manchu Empire and Qing China, 1600-1850* by Michael Fredholm von Essen